The Competition of Word-Formation Processes in the Derivational Paradigm of Verbs

Language and Text Studies

Edited by
Alexander Brock and Daniela Pietrini

Volume 21

PETER LANG

Cristina Fernández-Alcaina

The Competition of Word-Formation Processes in the Derivational Paradigm of Verbs

Diasynchronic Evidence for the Profile and Resolution of Competition in English

PETER LANG

Bibliographic Information published by the Deutsche Nationalbibliothek
The Deutsche Nationalbibliothek lists this publication in the Deutsche Nationalbibliografie; detailed bibliographic data is available online at http://dnb.d-nb.de.

Library of Congress Cataloging-in-Publication Data
A CIP catalog record for this book has been applied for at the Library of Congress.

This publication has been supported by the project FFI2017-89665-P, funded by the Spanish State Research Agency (SRA, Ministry of Science and Innovation) and by the European Regional Development Fund (ERDF).

ISSN 0941-4134
ISBN 978-3-631-86610-8 (Print)
E-ISBN 978-3-631-87289-5 (E-PDF)
E-ISBN 978-3-631-87290-1 (EPUB)
DOI 10.3726/b19408

Peter Lang – Berlin · Bern · Bruxelles · New York · Oxford · Warszawa · Wien

This publication has been peer reviewed.

www.peterlang.com

Contents

List of abbreviations

AmE	American English
BNC	*British National Corpus*
BrE	British English
COCA	*Corpus of Contemporary American English*
COHA	*Corpus of Historical American English*
EHCB	*English Historical Book Collection*
eOE	Early Old English
iWeb	*iWeb: The 14 Billion Word Web Corpus*
OE	Old English
OED	*Oxford English Dictionary*
OT	Optimality Theory
PPCEME	*Penn-Helsinki Parsed Corpus of Early Modern English*

Typographical conventions

Small capitals	semantic categories e.g., CAUSATIVE, RESULTATIVE, INSTRUMENT
Italics	dictionaries, terminology and examples in the running text e.g., *Collins*, *paradigm*, *mongrelize*
Single quotation marks	complete or partial lexicographic definitions of word senses e.g., *perfect* 'bring to perfection'
Boldface	emphasis within italics e.g., ***legal**ization*
Brackets	source of examples in the OED e.g., [1611 Speed *Hist. Gt. Brit*]

Introduction

Since *competition* is considered an 'inherent and universal feature of natural languages' (Štekauer 2017: 15), the definition of the term itself is often ambiguous, not just because it influences both language formation and interpretation, but because it obtains at all language levels, both synchronically and diachronically.

This book is concerned with competition at the level of morphology, in which the concept (also known as *rivalry*) has attracted much attention in research in the past years, as illustrated by the publication of several volumes, such as MacWhiney et al. (2014), Santana-Lario & Valera (2017) and Rainer et al. (2019), as well as by the papers on the topic presented at the *17th International Morphology Meeting* (Vienna 2016) and at the *Word-Formation Theories IV/ Typology and Universals in Word-Formation V* (Košice 2022) as part of the workshop 'Towards a competition-based word-formation theory'.

The study of competition in morphology usually goes hand in hand with the notion of *productivity* because competitors are typically contrasted according to their chance to decay or remain in use. In those cases where both competitors remain in language, they are contrasted according to their use, which is in turn measured according to their productivity. *Productivity* refers to the two related components of *availability* and *profitability* described by Corbin (1987: 177) and later accepted virtually unanimously.[1] Availability is therefore defined as the 'potential for repetitive rule-governed morphological coining' (Bauer 2001: 211). Once a morphological process is available, its profitability depends on the extent to which it can be used to create new words (Bauer 2001: 49).

Availability is a discrete variable conditioned by the language system; by contrast, profitability is a continuous variable conditioned by language norms (Bauer 2001: 209–210). The status of a form as *available* or *unavailable* depends on the properties of each language, often under the influence of its history and of its morphological model. Thus, for example, it has been claimed that it is the profile of English that makes the suffix *-ation* available with *-ize* verbs (e.g., *organization*), instead of *-ment* (e.g., **organizement*) (Bauer 2001: 205), even if it is not always possible to link up this type of constraints with specific factors of the morphological model, or to identify what specific factor constrains certain formations.

---

1 *Available* and *profitable* are the English translations suggested by Carstairs-McCarthy (1994) for Corbin's (1987) *disponible* and *rentable*.

This book focuses on the discrete dimension of productivity, that is, on the availability of forms and, specifically, in those cases in which there is competition and two or more forms are available as candidates to meet the same lexical need or to fill the same slot in the paradigm. The assumption is that co-existence may last for an indefinite period and may not exhibit any evident direction in its resolution for some time, but that it will eventually be resolved somehow. The profitability of each form or process may signal eventual resolutions, as described in Lara-Clares and Thompson (2019) for the competition of conversion and *-ness* suffixation in the formation of nouns for the expression of the semantic category STATIVE (e.g., *dark*^{N}/*darkness*). In this specific case, the results suggest that conversion prevails in the spoken mode, whereas *-ness* suffixation is preferred in the written mode (except for the subcategory *fiction*) (Lara-Clares & Thompson 2019: 46). This means that an additional variable needs to be considered for the description of competition: different modes, and perhaps also specialized domains or registers, may prime different forms or processes.

Even though we can speak of competition both in inflection (known as *overabundance*, Thornton 2012) and derivation, it is important to highlight that, although similarities exist, there are also differences in how competition operates in each morphological category. While inflection is determined by morphosyntax (Aronoff 2019), derivation is, in principle, driven by semantic needs. Therefore, neither the factors intervening nor the variables behind the resolution of competition are necessarily the same for inflection and derivation.

In the same way as competition is recognized for both inflection and derivation, the idea of a *paradigm* in derivation (or word formation) has gained ground in the past decades. Traditionally, research has focused on the description of the inflectional paradigm, as illustrated by the variety of theoretical perspectives from which it has been approached (see Boyé & Schalchli 2016 for a review). In derivation, conversely, the hypothesis of a paradigmatic organization has enjoyed much less attention based on its allegedly chaotic nature. Nevertheless, as Stump (2001: 65) notes, '[...] many of the arguments that motivate the postulation of paradigms in the inflectional domain have straightforward analogues in the domain of derivation'.

The growing interest in the derivational/word-formation paradigm is as well illustrated by a number of international conferences celebrated over the past years. Specifically, derivational paradigms were the topic of two international workshops at the 49th *SLE Conference* (Naples 2016) ('Paradigms in Word-Formation: New perspectives on data description and modelling' and 'Similarities and differences between inflectional and derivational paradigms: individual languages and beyond') and the workshop 'Revisiting paradigms in word-formation' at the *Word-Formation Theories III & Typology and Universals in Word-Formation* IV (Košice 2018), as well as in two editions of the international workshop *ParadigMo* (Toulouse 2017; Bordeaux 2021). The relevance of the topic is also evident from the number of specialized volumes and special issues recently published on the topic (Hathout & Namer 2018, 2019; Fernández-Domínguez et al. 2020; Körtvélyessy et al. 2020).

Despite the growing interest in the subject, the very definition of the term *paradigm* in derivation remains ambiguous, partly for its extended use in the literature and the variety of approaches that have addressed it. This is illustrated by the existence of a number of labels in descriptive linguistics: *word family* (Bauer & Nation 1993), *derivational family* (Roché 2009), or *derivational network* (Körtvélyessy et al. 2020), among others.

It is also unclear whether non-affixal processes should or even can be described in terms of paradigms, or as part and parcel of derivational paradigms. Štekauer (2014: 369) argues that only affixation can be considered in the derivational paradigm as '[…] it follows the requirement of systematic, regular and predictable relationships'.

The way in which word formation is paradigmatic is also theory-dependent. As noted by Bonami & Strnadová (2019), a group of approaches that draw on the Saussurean tradition employs the term *paradigmatic* for one of the two axes (as opposed to syntagmatic relations) of word formation (van Marle 1985). In a second group of approaches, *paradigmatic* refers to the set of forms that revolve around a common base, parallel to the type of organization described for inflection (Bauer 1997; Stump 2001; Beecher 2004; Štekauer 2014). As addressed in Section 1.3, this is also related to the two-fold nature of the term *competition* (i.e., between patterns/processes or between forms with the same base). Although few studies assess the relation between the two phenomena (Fernández-Alcaina & Čermák 2018; Fradin 2019), the results obtained suggest that an account of competition in the context of the paradigm where it occurs can provide better insights than when assessed in isolation.

The structure of the book is as follows: Chapter 1 reviews the most relevant research on the notions of *paradigm* and *competition*, with a special emphasis on the competition among verbalizing patterns and, specifically, conversion and affixation. Chapter 2 describes the method used for both the data collection and the data analysis of verbal competing clusters and their derivational paradigms. Chapter 3 presents an overview of the profile of competition and its resolution in both denominal and deadjectival verb formation. Since the number of competitors may affect the description of the profile of resolution, Chapter 4 addresses the competition in clusters with three forms (*triplets*) or above, and

Chapter 5 describes the competition in clusters with two members (*doublets*). Chapter 6 summarizes the main finding regarding the competition of verbal forms with the same base and how an analysis of the competitors in the context of the paradigms where they are allocated may in some cases provide additional evidence for the resolution of competition.

Chapter 1: Competition in derivational paradigms

1.1 Introduction

The notion of *paradigm* in morphology has been often described as a defining feature of inflection, in which, prototypically, the paradigm of a lexeme is a closed system where the filling of the cells is obligatory and where both form and content are related by means of one-to-one relations. Nevertheless, as Stump (2001: 65) notes, '[…] many of the arguments that motivate the postulation of paradigms in the inflectional domain have straightforward analogues in the domain of derivation'. This is the case of *competition*. To put it simply, *competition* is the situation in which two or more forms '[…] share some domain between them, producing outputs which, if acceptable, might fill the same functional slot in a paradigm' (Bauer et al. 2013: 568) either inflectional (e.g., *curriculum*.SG > *curricula*.PL/*curriculums*.PL, Quirk et al. 1985: 311) or derivational (e.g., *discriminative*/*discriminatory*, Kaunisto 2009: 74).

It is important to highlight, however, that although similarities exist, there are also differences in how competition operates in each morphological category. Such differences have important implications for the study of competition as neither the factors nor the variables behind the resolution of competition are necessarily the same for inflection and derivation. Specifically, Aronoff (2019: 55–56) notices two important differences in the competition between inflection and derivation. Because inflection is determined by morphosyntax, the number of forms that may occupy the same cell is usually limited. In contrast, since derivation is not obligatory, it is impossible to set a fixed number of potential competitors. Similarly, the factors that intervene in the resolution of competition may also vary. While differentiation between inflectional competitors can only be grounded on phonological or morphological reasons, these and other factors, including semantic and pragmatic ones, are at play in derivation, thus leading to a variety of profiles and outcomes of competition.

While previous research into the resolution of competition has usually focused on the study of the rival forms, the ways in which such co-existence may end and in which conditions are also in some way influenced by the rest of the members of the paradigm in which they are allocated. As several studies on standardization (Mal'ceva 1966; Gawełko 1977; Schupbach 1984, reviewed in

Pounder 2000: 83) suggest, the resolution of competition may be partly a consequence of the relations among the forms derived from a certain base.

This book is an attempt to shed light on the profile and resolution of competition in the derivational paradigms of English verbs. Before moving on to the empirical analysis and results, this chapter outlines the main findings of previous research.

1.2 Competition across history

The first references to competition can be found in the grammatical description of Sanskrit, in particular, in Pāṇini's *Astadhyayi*. The *Astadhyayi* consists of approximately 4,000 *sutras* ('aphorisms') ordered in a cyclic manner in which the application of a rule depends on its degree of specification, such that specific rules apply before general rules (Deo 2007: 187). Although Pāṇini did not directly address the concept of *competition*, the fact that grammar was rule-governed resulted in the formulation of grammatical exceptions also in terms of rules. Therefore, exceptions are not viewed as violations of rules but the result of the overlap of competing rules in a certain domain of application. This underlying principle was later explicitly formulated by Patañjali as the *Pāṇini's Principle*, which would set the bases for modern generativist approaches to morphology in the 20th century, such as the *Elsewhere Condition* (Anderson 1969; Kiparsky 1973), whereby the application of a general rule is overridden by the application of a more specific one, i.e., a specific rule blocks a general rule.

From a semantic perspective, competition has been seen as a necessary language condition to avoid synonymy. Bréal's (1897: 30) *loi de répartition* ('distribution law') states that '[…] les synonymes n'existent pas longtemps: ou bien ils se différencient, ou bien l'un des deux terms disparaît' ('synonyms do not exist for long: either they specialize or one of the two terms disappear', my translation). However, competition was not expected to reach an end immediately, as it takes time to be resolved. In this 'period of fluctuation' (Bréal 1897: 311), one of the competitors gradually replaces the other by restricting it to specific uses or, in some cases, forcing it out of the system and causing it to disappear as an available word (Bréal 1897: 311).[2]

Research into word formation carried out by the Neogrammarians also contributed to the study of morphological competition. The diachronic development

2 A detailed account on the development of the concept of competition across history is provided by Gardani et al. (2019).

of a certain category was first described by von Bahder (1880): his analysis of action nouns in German concludes that '[…] the rise and fall of synonymous patterns is often causally related' (Gardani et al. 2019: 9).

Competition between morphological processes was not directly addressed by Saussure in his *Cours*, but it was addressed by later structuralist scholars such as Benveniste (1948), for whom two completely synonymous patterns cannot co-exist. Similarly, Coseriu (1967) argued that the coining of certain forms may be prevented if either synonymous or homonymous forms already exist (Gardani et al. 2019: 12).

A more detailed account of competition from a structuralist perspective is provided by van Marle (1986). According to the *domain hypothesis*, the productivity of morphological processes is not only dependent on the structural and semantic properties of the forms that function as bases. Rather, productivity is also paradigmatically determined, because it is affected by competing processes that may occupy the same position in the system (van Marle 1986: 602).

Within the generativist framework, the notion of *competition* is central in the development of OT (Prince & Smolensky 1993). Broadly speaking, OT establishes that the observed forms of language are the result of the optimal resolution of the competition among several candidates. Although originally developed for phonology, OT was later implemented for morphology (Wunderlich 2001, in Gardani et al. 2019: 23). Since constraints in OT are hierarchically ordered, competition does not occur between rules themselves but between 'violable constraints' (Gardani et al. 2019: 24). Notably, Plag (1999) approached the productivity of verbalizing suffixation in Present-Day English from the point of view of OT.

Attempts to define the concept of competition in the last decades have also approached its definition from the point of view of evolutionary biology (Lindsay & Aronoff 2013; Aronoff 2016; Aronoff 2019). A parallelism between linguistic competition and Darwin's *Theory of Evolution* was already noticed by Bréal (1897: 310), when defining competition as a struggle for life. In particular, Aronoff (2019: 39) argues that complementary distribution is a consequence of Gause's (1934) *Competitive Exclusion Principle*, whereby the competition between two species for the same niche is always expected to come to an end, as one of them will prove more efficient than its counterpart. This reasoning holds not just for rival affixes, but for allomorphic variants too, as Aronoff (2019) views them as two sides of one phenomenon. In Aronoff's standpoint (2019: 44), allomorphs may be considered as rivals whose distribution is governed by Gause's *ecological niche differentiation*. The ecosystem metaphor is also used by Renner (2020) to refer to macro-level competition, in which the ten formal operations reviewed (prefixation, suffixation, compounding, blending, morphostasis, stress shift, clipping, desuffixation, initialization and replication) show a complementary distribution in the realization of four lexical functions, i.e., transcategorial, transconceptual, evaluative and compacting (Renner 2020: 9).

Regardless of other differences and similarities, what stands out from the shallow overview above is that the concept of *competition*, although widely recognized in language throughout history, still remains ambiguously defined. Therefore, in what follows, I will take the definition provided by Bauer et al. (2013) as a starting point, as it encompasses both inflection and derivation. In their view, competition is the situation in which two or more forms '[…] share some domain between them, producing outputs which, if acceptable, might fill the same functional slot in a paradigm (derivational or inflectional)' (Bauer et al. 2013: 568).

The definition of *competition* is also under the influence of the interaction between competition, productivity and blocking, among other factors (see Section 1.6). Partly due to the relative looseness of the term and also as a result of the strictness with which the conditions of synonymy and formal contrast may be applied, competition may be said to occur between various types of elements:

i) individual words (e.g., *songster* vs *chantress* 'female singer') (Bauer 2006: 182),
ii) patterns (e.g., *-ity* vs *-ness* in nominalizations), or
iii) processes (e.g., suffixation vs periphrastic expressions in the formation of comparative and superlative).

This book focuses on ii), that is, on the competition between patterns and, specifically, about verbalizing patterns that compete for the expression of the same meaning and attach to the same base (e.g., *pink*^{V}/*pinken* 'make pink'). The two approaches are described in more detail in Section 1.3.

1.3 Two approaches to competition

1.3.1 Competition between patterns

Broadly speaking, *competition* may refer to the catalog of patterns (or, at a higher level, processes) available for the formation of a word, in which the selection of one or the other patterns is guided by a series of restrictions (e.g., phonetic, formal, semantic, etc.). From a paradigmatic perspective to word formation, the restrictions governing the selection of a particular pattern may be described in terms of domains. *Derivational domains* are defined as the sets of words that may act as bases for the members of a certain morphological category (van Marle

1985, 1986).[3] Specifically, van Marle (1985: 195) argues that '[...] derivational domains of morphological categories may be determined to a greater or lesser extent by paradigmatic forces', without the need to resort to the existence of blocking-devices that prevent the coinage of words such as **furiosity* due to the existence of already attested words such as *fury* (Aronoff 1976). In this respect, van Marle (1985: 195) states that:

> What should be emphasized in this connection is, that this 'hindering' force of rival forms is paradigmatic in nature. For, the coining of *furiosity* and *decentness* is impeded by forces that are radiated by other words in the system. It is the relations between elements in absentia which underline the non-occurrence of **furiosity* and **decentness.*

Van Marle (1985) distinguishes between general and specific cases and argues that '[i]t is the productivity of the general cases which may be affected by paradigmatic forces' (van Marle 1985: 199). Thus, and following the example provided by van Marle (1985) , English pluralization is governed by paradigmatic forces in that the general case (suffix *-s*, e.g., *cow > cows*) applies in all the domains where the special cases (e.g., *-en*, as in *ox > oxen*) do not apply. However, the dichotomy productive/ general and unproductive/specific may not be this simple, since special cases may be productive too. This is illustrated by Dutch pluralization, where the special case (i.e., the suffix *-s*) is productive in certain domains (e.g., foreign words such as *memo > memos*), where the general case (i.e., the suffix *-en*) does not apply.

Van Marle (1985, 1986) also distinguishes two types of special cases: systematic and non-systematic. While special cases are rule-governed (i.e., by type), non-systematic special cases are lexically governed (i.e., by token) (Plag 1999: 52–53). Thus, the former affects the properties of the domain of the general case, but the latter affects only the actuation of the general case (van Marle 1986: 607).

In this sense of *paradigmatic*, it is by means of opposite relations that competing patterns are distributed into derivational domains. Therefore, competition becomes a driving force for the configuration of the morphological system.

Regarding the research into the competition between verbalizing patterns in English, few studies deal with affix rivalry. Those tackling the topic of affix

---

3 The view of word formation as a system where rival affixes are organized into domains contrasts with an approach to productivity in terms of constraints (e.g., phonological, morphological, semantic, etc.). Plag (1999: 54) argues that, in the case of the rivalry between verbalizing affixes, the distribution '[...] is not governed by primarily paradigmatic forces', but rather in terms of the individual syntagmatic properties of each affix, together with token-blocking and certain cases of local analogy (Plag 1999: 234). Both approaches may be seen as equivalent (Bauer et al. 2013: 578).

competition focus mainly on the identification of the factors that are assumed to account for the resolution of such competition (Schneider 1987; Plag 1999; Kjellmer 2001; Gottfurcht 2008; Bauer et al. 2010). However, neither the range of affixes described nor the factors identified are consistent from author to author. This leads to a blurred picture of what matters in the resolution of affix competition in verbal derivation. In what follows I will briefly summarize the main studies on verbal competition in terms of the affixes considered and the factors described as major influences on the distribution of the affixes.

Regarding the units analysed, competing affixes have received uneven attention. Some studies have researched groups of two or three affixes, e.g., Schneider (1987) only considers the suffixes *-en*, *-ify* and *-ize*, Bauer et al. (2010) address the competition between deadjectival *-en* suffixation and conversion, and Fernández-Alcaina (2017) focuses on the competition between *-ize* suffixation and conversion in verbs derived from the same base. More comprehensive studies are available by Plag (1999), Kjellmer (2001) and Gottfurcht (2008), although not all the possibilities for verbal derivation are contemplated in them. Plag (1999) discusses the competition between conversion and *-ate*, *-ify* and *-ize* suffixation in Present-Day English; Kjellmer (2001) and Gottfurcht (2008) approach competition among affixes from a diachronic perspective, even if Kjellmer (2001) excludes conversion from his analysis and Gottfurcht (2008) limits the study of competition to denominal verbs.

In terms of the restrictions considered, the diversity and relevance of the factors proposed in the literature on the competition in verbal derivation suggest that they are highly theory-dependent: Plag (1999) analyses the productivity of verbal affixes (and conversion) within the framework of OT and concludes that phonological and semantic factors can account for the distribution of verbal affixes (Plag 1999: 228). Gottfurcht (2008: 182–211) suggests that derivation is influenced by semantic factors and by frequency-related factors, as well as by the interaction between the verb-formation processes. Specifically, she argues that, even though all the semantic categories are possible for all the processes analysed in denominal derivation, they are not available to the same degree: while *be-* and conversion are more likely to appear in an ORNATIVE structure, *-ify* and *-ize* are preferred for RESULTATIVE interpretations, *en-* usually expresses the categories LOCATIVE or ORNATIVE, and *-ate* ORNATIVE or RESULTATIVE (Gottfurcht 2008: 205). Furthermore, in Gottfurcht's thesis, derivation is also influenced by what she termed the *Semantic Category Distribution Effect*, defined as the phenomenon in which '[n]ative speakers are sensitive to the semantic category distribution of existing lexical items derived by the denominal verb formation processes and use this information when creating novel denominal verbs' (Gottfurcht 2008: 72).

A systematic assessment of a series of factors possibly at play in competition is provided by Schneider (1987), Kjellmer (2001) and, to a lesser extent, Bauer et al. (2010). The results obtained, however, appear to be mostly inconclusive. While Schneider (1987) provides a systematic account of the extra-linguistic, phonological, morphological and semantic factors influencing the competition between *-en*, *-ify* and *-ize* suffixation, he does not comment further upon the reasons underlying such generalizations (Plag 1999: 93). Both Kjellmer (2001) and Bauer et al. (2010), in contrast, elaborate on the influence the factors reviewed have on the resolution of competition in deadjectival derivation. Kjellmer (2001) concludes that, of all the factors considered, only the etymology and derivational history of the base as well as its frequency are 'of great significance' (Kjellmer 2001: 170), while the semantics of the base turns to be 'inconsequential' (Kjellmer 2001: 170). Similar conclusions are drawn by Bauer et al. (2010) regarding the semantics of the base. In the latter case's assessment of phonological and frequency-related factors, the results obtained also suggest that deadjectival derivation may lead to 'unpredictable classes, and that standardization is not leading to a situation in which the distribution of the competing process can be predicted' (Bauer et al. 2010: 15).

1.3.2 Competition between forms with the same base

From a more restrictive perspective, *competition* may refer to those cases in which two or more synonymous forms sharing the same base but with a different affix are attested in language. They are the result of an overlap in the restrictions that govern the distribution of patterns. Such overlap is materialized as the coexistence of two or more forms within the same slot in the derivational paradigm.

A more fine-grained definition of this type of competition is described by Fradin (2019: 68), who lists four conditions that must be satisfied in order for competition to occur, as e.g., in *encadrage/encadrement* 'framing' (Fradin 2019: 78):

i) distinct exponent,
ii) same base,
iii) same semantic content, and
iv) same syntactic distribution.

However, even if forms may share the same meaning, free variation is rare and doublets also need to be correlated with the same construction and have the same distribution to be considered as true instances of competition. As it may be expected, once doublets are closely analysed, the number of true cases of competition decreases sharply: '[...] their distribution often presents differences that might subsequently become institutionalized meaning distinctions' (Fradin 2019: 90).

In this line, I have defined competition elsewhere as '[...] the co-existence of two or more affixes for the same base and for the expression of the same semantic category, if restrictions (e.g., phonological, morphological) do not apply and no semantic or distributional differences are observed' (Fernández-Alcaina 2017: 166). Furthermore, based on the assumption that the various meanings of a form '[...] may be assessed independently for availability and profitability' (Bauer 2001: 211), competition is always considered to occur between particular senses of two or more forms. Research into nominal doublets in Present-Day English concludes that competition in pairs needs to be assessed individually (cf. Lara-Clares 2017 on the competition between nouns derived by conversion and by *-ation* suffixation).

The resolution of competition in doublets is not clear either, and some pairs where the same affixes are in competition usually show different patterns of resolution. Research into nominal doublets in Old English reveals that neither morphological factors nor the semantics of the base can completely account for the outcome of the resolution of competition (Amutio-Palacios 2013). These results lead to the conclusion that it is possible to speak only in terms of 'tendencies', rather than rules, in the direction of the resolution of competition (Amutio-Palacios 2013: 60).

Similarly, the results obtained in the competition between *-ive*/*-ory* adjectives exhibit a high degree of heterogeneity regarding both how competition is resolved and the dominance of one or the other suffix (Kaunisto 2009). In this line, the study of the diachronic competition between adjectival doublets in *-some* and *-able* (e.g., *laughable*/*laughsome*, Smith 2020: Section 3.3) reveals that the decrease in the productivity of *-some* suffixation may be the result of a series of factors, such as the existence of synonymous affixes (e.g., *-ish*, *-ful*, *-able*, etc.) or lexicalization and fossilization (Smith 2020: paragraph 97).

The influence of pragmatic factors on the resolution of competition in doublets and triplets is nonetheless more difficult to account for, as some competitors are commonly used interchangeably, e.g., *studentdom*/*studenthood*/*studentship* 'the state or condition of being a student' (Bauer et al. 2013: 260). Empirical research on register distribution observed in nominal doublets in Present-Day English (Lara-Clares 2017; Lara-Clares & Thompson 2019) shows that the distribution of a certain affix may vary depending on the competitor and the category expressed. Overall, conversion may prevail in all registers when in competition with *-ation* suffixation for the category ACTION (e.g., *dispute/disputation*; Lara-Clares 2017: 224). However, the same process (conversion) exhibits a trend to specialization in the spoken mode when in competition with *-ness* suffixation for the category STATIVE, e.g., *dark/darkness* (Lara-Clares & Thompson 2019: 17, 21).

In summary, the existence of doublets has been admitted to be less common than assumed (Plag 1999; Kaunisto 2009; Fernández-Alcaina 2017; Fradin 2019), and the results arising from the resolution of competition in doublets appear to be unclear too.

Compared to the competition among verbalizing patterns, little attention has been paid to cases where restrictions overlap, i.e., doublets and triplets. Even if doublets are argued to contribute to a better delimitation of the constraints influencing productivity (Romaine 2004: 1638), their treatment in the literature is uneven. To the best of my knowledge, only Plag (1999) and Gottfurcht (2008) devote a section to the existence of verbal doublets (but not to triplets). Even here, little is said about how competition is resolved. In fact, both authors reach opposite conclusions regarding the status of competitors with the same base in derivation. Plag (1999) argues that competition occurs in language to a lesser extent than previously thought and that, as a consequence, the number of true competitors, i.e., those derived from the same base, is reduced, at least in the case of the neologisms coined in the 20th century. In contrast, Gottfurcht (2008: 209) concludes that '[…] denominal verb formation processes are *always* in competition, unless of course the process is all but dead and gone for English' (Gottfurcht 2008: 209) (emphasis as in the original). Regarding competitors with the same base and different affixes, she argues that, from a diachronic perspective, the large number of 'multiplets' with the same base underline the frequency with which competition occurs, even if they did not get to survive into Present-Day English (Gottfurcht 2008: 210). Specifically, Gottfurcht (2008) identifies 698 sets of verbs where the latest-attested item has a sense that competes with one of the senses of a previously attested form (Gottfurcht 2008: 196). Still, it is unclear how the resolution in the sets of competitors with the same base analysed takes place. It is also ambiguous whether there exists a difference between the sets of verbs where the second element has been '[…] created to compete with another existing verb' (e.g., *stone/stonify* 'turn into stone', Gottfurcht 2008: 196) and those where volition is implied in the creation of a form '[…] that is now better able to trigger the desired semantic association' (Gottfurcht 2008: 202).

The resolution of competition in verbal derivation has been explored in previous research (Fernández-Alcaina 2017), although it was limited to the analysis of verbs derived by *-ize* suffixation or by conversion, e.g., *ghetto/ghettoize* 'put into a ghetto'. The results obtained show that competition is resolved in most doublets either by the obsolescence of one of the competitors (e.g., *savage/savagize*) or, to a lesser extent, by semantic specialization (e.g., *tender* keeps the general meaning 'make tender', while *tenderize* is mostly used to referring to food as 'make (food) tender'), or according to variety (e.g., *quiet* seems to be preferred in AmE while *quieten* is more common in BrE). Clusters where the two competitors have become obsolete were also attested (e.g., *melancholy/melancholize*). However, over 35 % of the 45 clusters analysed in that study were attested to be in ongoing competition according to OED data. Further research on the paradigms created around the verb in competition (Fernández-Alcaina & Čermák 2018) shows that, at least for some of the groups of the competitors analysed, the study of their derivatives may prompt at a consistent direction in the resolution of competition. In any case, the conclusions drawn should be taken with caution, as the number of clusters analysed was low.

1.4 Derivational paradigms and competition

1.4.1 Paradigms in morphology

Paradigms can be loosely defined as 'sets of related words' based on 'paradigmatic relationships' (van Marle 1994: 2927) but, due to the pervasiveness of the term in linguistics, there is not a unique definition for the concept.

The first references to the concept of a paradigm date back to the Old-Babylonian tradition, where records show that the paradigm was already described as a list of inflected forms from a word (usually a verb) (Campbell 2002: 82). However, it was not until Classical Greece that paradigms started to be described as occupying a central role in language description. Aristotle first defined the word 'as the smallest meaningful part of a unit' where 'the parts contribute to the meaning of the whole, yet [...] they have not an independent meaning' (*De Interpretiatione* 16b, 27–36 in Blevins 2013: 377). Words were distinguished by the *ptōsis* ('fall') but no meaningful sub-word units were recognized. Therefore, the formation of new words (and word-forms) took place through the formal modification of a basic form (Robins 2000: 53). These processes were extended to other language phenomena through proportional analogy, based on the regular patterns represented by exemplary paradigms. The study of morphology in the 19th century and the beginning of the 20th century still largely relied on the Classical models, specifically on Aristotle's view of the word as the basic unit and of analogy as a driving force within paradigms.

That said, any attempt to define the term *paradigm* inevitably goes back to Saussure's (1959[1916]) associative relations,[4] defined as sets of items related by some shared feature (the radical) and representing various linguistic realities. In particular, Saussure distinguishes four types of relations, three of which are of special interest here insofar as they capture the senses in which the term is most frequently used in the literature. Thus, *paradigm* may refer to a set of forms:

i) with a common stem (e.g., *enseignement* 'teaching^{N}', *enseigner* 'to teach'),
ii) sharing a common affix (e.g., *enseignement* 'teaching^{N}', *changement* 'change'), or
iii) expressing the same semantic category (e.g., *enseignement* 'teaching^{N}', *éducation* 'education').[5]

The non-specificity of Saussure's relations shows in the ambiguity with which the term appears in the literature a century later, where no unified interpretation of the concept stands out. Paradigms have been traditionally restricted to the field of inflection, where the formation of new word-forms was considered highly regular and predictable, in contrast to the seeming irregularity of derivational morphology. However, research in the last decades has provided both morphological and psycholinguistic evidence for the existence of paradigms in word formation too, even if they do not necessarily share all the features previously described for inflectional paradigms.

Most perspectives focus on providing evidence for the role played by paradigms in affixation, since the relations among the members of the paradigm need to be regular and predictable. The idea of a paradigm that encompasses all word-formation processes has been considered '[...] vacuous because it does not lead to a predictable and regularly organized system of complex words' (Štekauer 2014: 369).

1.4.2 Paradigms in word formation

In the onomasiological tradition, word formation is a system where parts are paradigmatically related and where motivation is key. However, relations cannot be reduced to those established between the motivating (basic form) and the motivated words, but they often exhibit a higher degree of complexity. In this

4 The term *paradigmatic* was later introduced by Hjelmslev (Harder 1996: 439 in Nielsen 2016: 157) to draw a distinction between the syntagmatic and the paradigmatic axes. This is the term employed henceforth here.

5 Examples i) to iii) are my translation of Saussure's (1959 [1916]: 126).

view, the word-formation system is formed by both a syntagmatic (derivational series) and a paradigmatic (derivational paradigm) dimension, which together form the so-called derivational nest. Specifically, *derivational series* are defined as 'sequences of consecutive motivation pairs' (Körtvélyessy et al. 2020: 3), while derivational paradigms are networks of complex words organized around a common basic (motivating) word.

Similarly, in van Marle's (1985) *Paradigmatic Derivational Morphology*, complex words are not seen as the outputs resulting from the application of rules, but as part of a system based on the notion of *relatedness*, i.e., based on the similarities and differences among the members that form the networks (van Marle 1985). Thus, rather than on the relations between base and derivatives, the focus is on the relations established among complex words.

Van Marle (1985) thus draws a distinction between the derivational paradigm and the paradigmatic axis of word formation based on the notion of *morphological category*, defined as 'a series of words sharing identical formal feature and identical semantic feature', e.g., *groenig* 'greenish', *kalig* 'baldish', *nattig* 'wettish', *zoetig* 'sweetish' (van Marle 1985: 88–89). As van Marle (1985) notes, the main difference between the derivational paradigm and the paradigmatic axis of word formation lies in the distinction between base and morphological category. Therefore, while the members of derivational paradigms are derived from a common base (e.g., *groen* > *groen-erig* > *groenig-or*, van Marle 1985: 126), in van Marle's approach paradigms are organized in terms of morphological categories (e.g., *groen* > *groen-st*/*groenig-st*/*groenachtig-st*, van Marle 1985: 126).

The semantic feature common to the formal realization shared by the members of the morphological category is referred to as the *categorial value* (van Marle 1985: 89). In this sense, the same semantic distinction between *groen* and *groenig* is found between those pairs formed by the same pattern: *kaal*/*kalig*, *nat*/*nattig* or *zoet*/*zoetig*. Van Marle (1985: 155, 1994: 2928) distinguishes four groups of categories, depending on whether the members of the category share:

i) a common morphological base (e.g., a noun, adjective or verb),
ii) a common base and the same semantic properties, thus resulting in rival morphological categories (e.g., past tense in English can be expressed either by the suffix *-ed*, as in *work* > *worked*, or by vowel alternation, as in *swim* > *swam*),
iii) a common base and similar (but not identical) semantic properties, e.g., adjectives in Dutch may be formed by attaching the suffixes *-ig* and *-erig* (e.g., *groenig*/*groenerig*), but the latter has a stronger 'subjectively appreciative' meaning, and

iv) a common affix, but not necessarily the same base, e.g., the suffix *-ize* can form verbs both from nouns (e.g., *alphabetize*) and adjectives (e.g., *fertilize*).

A similar distinction between paradigms formed around a common base and a common category is found in Lexical Morphology (Roché 2009), where two types of paradigms are distinguished: *derivational families* and *derivational series*. The combination of both types forms the *paradigmatic system*, defined as 'a collection of (partial) families that are aligned in terms of the content-based relations that their members entertain' (Bonami & Strnadová 2019: 169).

Derivational families, as paradigms, are sets of forms that share the same base (e.g., ***legal***, ***legal***_ize_, ***legal***_ization_). They may be defined then as (subparts of) derivational paradigms that are organized as networks characterized by containing a fixed number of cells.

By contrast, derivational series are sets of forms derived through the same pattern (e.g., *actual/actualize, random/randomize, sterile/sterilize*), which goes in line with van Marle's (1985) notion of morphological category. Unlike inflection, where morphosyntactic features are inherent to the form, derivation relies on external evidence, i.e., linguistic context. Therefore, depending on the construction where they occur, the same unit may give rise to two distinct derivational series, as in the examples below (Fradin 2018: 166):

étayer$_1$	'to underpin'	>	*étaiement*$_1$	'underpinning'
rapiécer$_1$	'to patch'	>	*rapiécement*$_1$	'action of patching'
renforcer$_1$	'to reinforce'	>	*renforcerment*$_1$	'reinforcement'
étayer$_2$	'to underpin'	>	*étaiement*$_2$	'prop'
rapiécer$_2$	'to patch'	>	*rapiécement*$_2$	'patch'
renforcer$_2$	'to reinforce'	>	*renforcerment*$_2$	'what reinforces'

Both derivational families and derivational series have an effect on word formation too (Roché 2011: 87) and, hence, in competition, as shown by recent research on French nominalizations (Fradin 2019). The relation between paradigms and morphological competition is further elaborated in Section 1.4.3.

1.4.3 Competition within derivational paradigms

Most studies addressing the competition between forms with the same base usually focus on the competitors themselves. However, as Pounder (2000: 83) notes, historical studies on standardization in Russian (Mal'ceva 1966; Schupbach 1984) and French (Gawełko 1977) have shown that the resolution of competition is '[…] at least partly dependent on relations holding between the complete set of lexemes related to the same base'. Once two forms with the same base enter the system, the choice for one or the other takes place, in many cases, 'at the level of the individual lexical paradigm' (Pounder 2000: 697). However, to the best of my knowledge, few studies have addressed the relation between competition and paradigms, partly due to the problems relating to the very identification of semantic differences in doublets (Bonami & Strnadová 2019: 176).

In his assessment of the competition between nominalizations in *-age* and *-ment* in French, Fradin (2019: 88) concludes that 'the competition of derivational forms can only be assessed against the entailments triggered by their distribution'. While this is true for ongoing competition (see Lara-Clares 2017; Lara-Clares & Thompson 2019), the use of historical corpora for the identification and analysis of diachronic competition has returned few results.

When differences in the distribution of two forms '[…] might subsequently become institutionalized meaning distinctions' (Fradin 2019: 90), they may become part of the meaning of the competing forms, thus making possible the distinction of different series and, at a more abstract level, the distinction of different patterns which are in complementary distribution. For example, in French nominalizations, the preference for a specific suffix is dependent on the distinction control/non-control in the base meaning: while *-age* usually attaches to bases involving control, *-ment* nominalizations are built upon bases involving lack of control (Fradin 2019: 85). This does not imply that overlaps do not exist, because competition may take time to result in a given outcome.

Regarding derivational families, their effect is especially evident where each meaning is linked to a distinct exponent, i.e., canonical derivation (Corbett 2010). However, derivational paradigms do not often behave in this way. In fact, the extent to which paradigms have an effect is hindered by 'the profusion of constructs in attested families' (Fradin 2019: 86).

Since such distinctions in the base form may be inherited by its derivatives,[6] the analysis of derivational paradigms of two competing forms may contribute insights into the resolution of competition in favor of one of the competing forms (Fernández-Alcaina & Čermák 2018: 93). Specifically, previous research into the competition between conversion and *-ize* suffixation in causative verbs

6 However, this is not always the case as both narrowing and widening of the base senses are also attested (Bauer & Valera 2015).

shows that the allocation of doublets within their respective paradigms presents advantages for the study of competition in two ways.

First, considering paradigms provides further evidence concerning the outcomes of competition. As noted by Fernández-Alcaina & Čermák (2018: 79), the comparison of the results obtained to those from a previous study on competition (Fernández-Alcaina 2017) shows that it is possible to obtain more fine-grained results when the derivational paradigm is considered. In particular, of the 15 out of 45 clusters classified as exhibiting ongoing competition in a previous study (Fernández-Alcaina 2017), 13 clusters were reclassified as instances of resolved competition once paradigms were considered. Of those 13 clusters, *-ize* suffixation was preferred in seven clusters, while conversion was found to prevail over *-ize* suffixation in three clusters. The resulting picture suggests that there is a slight bias towards *-ize* instead of towards conversion.

Second, the earliest attestation dates of the derivatives may also provide evidence for the features displayed by the clusters where competition is resolved. Specifically, a diachronic analysis of the competition shows that there is an increasing preference over time for *-ize* suffixation over conversion to express causative verbs. However, such preference does not prevent the existence of clusters where the converted verb is preferred. In the latter case, it has been observed that, based on the earliest attestation dates of their derivatives, '[…] once a causative zero-derived verb has derivatives mapping on this sense, *-ize* verbs are less likely to replace them, and thus, the subparadigm of the zero-derived competitor seems to support a preference for its base' (Fernández-Alcaina & Čermák 2018: 89). Further research including other patterns may yield a more complete picture of the competition in verbal domain.

1.5 The resolution of competition

Various scenarios have been described in the literature with regard to how competition is resolved, often under different labels. In this section I use the terminology employed by Moravcsik (2014) (although references to other authors are made when relevant), except that I restrict its use to morphological competition. Therefore, the ways in which resolution may occur is limited to four possibilities: *separation*, *compromise*, *override* and *deadlock* (Moravcsik 2014: 2–3). They are briefly described below:

i) *Separation* occurs whenever there is no overlap in the domains of two or more 'motivations' (in Moravcsik's words), e.g., the verbs *winterize*/*winter* do not exhibit competing senses as the former means 'prepare something for use in cold weather', while *winter* means 'keep or maintain during winter'.

ii) *Deadlock* (also called *blocking*) occurs if two or more principles do not apply and, thus, no output arises (Moravcsik 2014: 2–3), e.g., the existence of *thief* ('someone who steals') pre-empts **stealer*, at least in British English, when they have the same meaning.[7]

Neither *separation* nor *deadlock* are true outcomes of the type of competition addressed here, because they do not imply preliminary co-existence. Therefore, I will focus on the outcomes of *compromise* and *override* and how they operate at a morphological level:

iii) *Compromise* (also called *differentiation* by Aronoff 2016) occurs if two forms overlap in meaning for some time but one of them ends up specializing in a distinct domain. In other words, competition is resolved through semantic specialization, a process which is well-attested in the literature (Fowler 1928, in Plag 1999; Bauer 2006; Kaunisto 2009; Bauer et al. 2013: 580; Lindsay & Aronoff 2013; Fernández-Alcaina 2017), e.g., the adjectives *discriminatory* and *discriminative* were originally synonymous forms meaning 'relating to making distinctions'. Corpus data suggest that the form *discriminatory* has negative connotations, whereas *discriminative* conveys, in most cases, a neutral meaning (Kaunisto 2009: 83).

iv) *Override* (also called *extinction* by Aronoff 2016) refers to the situation in which one of the forms outlives its competitor, leading to the obsolescence of the latter (e.g., Bauer 2006; Kaunisto 2009; Fernández-Alcaina 2017), e.g., *mongrel* (1602–1662)[8]/*mongrelize* (1629–1999) 'make mongrel in breed'. In most cases, the form with the earliest attestation date is the best candidate to prevail over the other. Exceptions are also attested, e.g., the adjective *regulative* is attested much earlier than its competitor *regulatory*, but it is the form in *-ory* that exhibits a higher frequency in Present-Day English (Kaunisto 2009: 85). Whichever way, competition is resolved in some way in favor of some of the forms, even if '[...] victory may be temporary' (Aronoff 2016;

---

7 However, as Bauer (2001: 136–137) notes, *stealer* may be used in compounds such as *sheep-stealer* (but not **sheep-thief*). This particularity stresses the importance of addressing competition among senses, also in line with Díaz-Negrillo (2017), Lara-Clares (2017), Lara-Clares & Thompson (2019) and this analysis.

8 The latest attestation date holds, even if an attestation of the form *mongreled* (1941) dates back to the 20th century. This is because the lack of evidence between the 17th and the 20th century may be due to missing written records or may be a case of *renewed availability* (Bauer 2014). According to Allan (2012: 25), however, the lack of attestation records cannot be considered as 'evidence for lack of use'.

cf. also Bauer et al. 2010 on patterns in verb derivation changing over time), e.g., in the cluster *melancholy/melancholize*, the attestation dates indicate that the converted form outlived its competitor in *-ize* for some time, but it ceased to be in use early in the 19th century (Fernández-Alcaina 2017).[9]

Even if resolution is always expected to occur, two or more competitors may also be in a situation of *equilibrium* (Aronoff 2016, after Gause's axiom), where competition remains unresolved for some time (Bauer 2006; Kaunisto 2009: 86; Fernández-Alcaina 2017), e.g., *acronym* (1967)/*acronymize* (1955) 'convert into an acronym'. This is particularly common in the forms that start to compete in the 20th century, simply because competition may take time to be resolved. In fact, as Bauer (2006: 190) explains, since so many new forms were created and borrowed into English in the 17th century, '[...] the history of the past 300 years of English morphology is a reaction against the plethora of potential processes arising from the introduction of overwhelming loan morphology'.

Although the set of outcomes of competition is logically limited to the set of possibilities described above, the direction in which competition is usually resolved is unclear. In fact, the results obtained regarding the patterns of resolution are often uneven, even if competition occurs between two specific affixes. Thus, in the competition of adjectives in *-ic/-ical* (Kaunisto 2007) and *-ory/-ive* (Kaunisto 2009), resolution is either by semantic specialization or by the obsolescence of one of the forms. This does not imply that resolution always occurs in favor of the same affix, e.g., in the cluster *compulsive/compulsory*, the *-ory* adjective keeps the original meaning 'obligatory' and corners its *-ive* competitor to a different semantic niche (Kaunisto 2009: 81–82). In contrast, the *-ive* adjective in the cluster *investigative/investigatory* shows a higher frequency in corpus data (Kaunisto 2009: 84). Examples like these show that, while it is possible to list the distinct outcomes of competition, the reasons behind such resolution are in some cases unclear, as two apparently similar clusters may resolve in favor of different forms.

9 The form *melancholied* is recorded in a quotation from 1980 where it specifies that there is no form *melancholied* that can be used as a paraphrase of 'cause somebody to become melancholic': *There is no transitive 'melancholied' that would give 'John melancholied Bill' as a paraphrase of 'John caused Bill to become melancholy'* [1980 *Jrnl. Philos.* 77 299].

1.6 Limitations in the study of competition

A number of variables need to be considered in any study of competition, especially if this is done from a diachronic perspective. What follows is an outline of the main aspects that play a role in competition.

1.6.1 Frequency and productivity

Productivity and *competition* are interlinked concepts that need to be revised jointly, because the latter is both the cause and the consequence of changes in productivity (Gottfurcht 2008 or Scherer 2015: 5, and Bauer et al. 2010: 11, respectively).

When two processes are in competition, changes in the productivity of one of them may produce changes in the productivity of its competitor (Scherer 2015: 5). The extent to which these changes may influence productivity depends on the nature of the competitors: the availability of a form derived by a certain word-formation process replacing an existing lexical form may increase the productivity of the word-formation process.

When competition occurs between two or more patterns, the impact it may have on productivity is even greater, causing the total or partial unavailability of one of the patterns in some cases. Thus, e.g., some OE nouns derived by *-ness* nouns were in the ME period and later replaced *-ity* nouns, e.g., *cristeness/christianity* (Riddle 1985: 447).

1.6.2 Lexicalization

The study of competition also requires the consideration of the role played by lexicalization, as the resulting loss of transparency obscures the separation between available and unavailable processes. However, measuring the extent to which lexicalization influences productivity and, therefore, competition is complex, among other reasons because, as Bauer (1983: 98) points out, '[…] there is not necessarily an influence in one direction only'. Further, competitors based on the same patterns may be influenced differently by lexicalization, as illustrated by the comparison of doublets such as *barbaric/barbarous* and *cupric/cuprous*, where the meaning of the second pair of competitors has become lexicalized (Bauer et al. 2013: 577).

1.6.3 Borrowing

The effect of language contact on morphology is widely illustrated by the competition between native and non-native affixes, where the introduction of the latter type may gradually modify the productivity of its native counterpart. This does not necessarily imply the obsolescence of the native process since affixes may become specialized. Arndt-Lappe (2014) notes that, while *-ness* is synchronically considered as the default option to derive abstract nouns, a diachronic analysis of its competition with the suffix *-ity* shows that the latter has increasingly gained ground in certain morphological domains.

Specialization may also occur based on semantic differences. As pointed out by Bauer et al. (2013: 284), '[…] it is more common for conversion to express a non-causative meaning', which is in line with later research into CAUSATIVE doublets in *-ize* suffixation compared with conversion (Fernández-Alcaina 2017). The results obtained suggest that the 18th century's increase in the number of verbs in *-ize* was accompanied by a tendency for converted competitors to become obsolete or semantically specialized with a non-causative sense (Fernández-Alcaina 2017: 202). Nevertheless, even if studies on competition need to account for the role played by borrowing, the importance of its influence on the resolution of competition remains unanswered.

Yet in some other cases, as remarked by Nevalainen (1999), distinguishing borrowings from English coinages is not always without difficulty, because lexicographic data supply unclear information regarding their etymological origins. When *reborrowing* of the same form but with a different sense occurs, it is also difficult to decide whether this new sense is a consequence of meaning extension or it has been borrowed from the donor language (Nevalainen 1999).

1.6.4 Blocking

Aronoff (1976: 43) first defined *blocking* as 'the non-occurrence of one form due to the simple existence of another'. Since then, the concept has been widely used in the literature about competition and productivity, even if the role it plays is still a matter of discussion. As Bauer et al. (2013: 575) argue, '[i]f there can be competition between morphological processes on the same base, there can be no blocking'. By contrast, if we consider that it is not the production of a new form that is prevented by blocking but its institutionalization in the speech community (Bauer et al. 2013: 576), then it has been argued that at least some types of blocking may be relevant for the study of competition (Plag 1999).

The first distinction in the definition of blocking is drawn between *blocking by homonymy* and *blocking by synonymy* (Bauer et al. 2013: 575). Blocking by homonymy refers to the loss of certain forms due to the existence of another word with the same form and distinct meaning in order to avoid ambiguity, e.g., the unavailability of **to fall* in analogy with *to summer* or *to winter* because of the existence of *to fall* 'to drop'.

Blocking by synonymy has received much attention in research. Rainer (1988) distinguishes two types of blocking according to the nature of the units: *token-blocking* refers to the blocking of a particular form due to the existence of a synonymous word, e.g.,*?stealer/thief*; in contrast, *type-blocking* involves the competition of two word-formation processes, e.g., *-ity/-ness.*

Studies on competition find opposite results regarding the pressure exerted by each type of blocking. Plag (1999: 234) argues that only token-blocking and local analogy are at play in Present-Day English verbal competition. Similar conclusions are drawn by Lindsay & Aronoff (2013, based on diachronic evidence), because it indicates a gradual replacement of *ness* suffixation in certain domains in favor of *-ity*, therefore implying that type-blocking does not prevent a less productive affix to be preferred in certain domains.

1.6.5 Analogy

Although the role played by analogy has been extensively discussed in the literature on productivity, few studies on competition include it as a factor. Plag (2000) argues that, alongside type-blocking, local analogy is one of the two mechanisms that can influence affix selection.

Yet, the vagueness with which analogy is treated is well reflected by Kaunisto (2007: 38), who refers to it as 'a desire towards harmony' when considering analogy as a possible mechanism at play in the creation of *-ical* adjectives relating to 'knowledge'. On the same page, however, Kaunisto (2007: 38) accepts that '[...] the significance of this factor remains a mere theoretical possibility, as its effect is difficult to verify with absolute certainty'.

Other authors ascribe a more central position to analogy in the discussion about competition between affixes. Arndt-Lappe (2014) analyses the competition between *-ity* and *-ness* from an analogy-based perspective and concludes that analogy is particularly relevant for identifying differences in the productivity of competitors.

1.7 Summary

Competition is a pervasive process and a relationship that affects all levels of language. In particular, its existence in morphology was already noticed by Sanskrit grammarians and dealt with from a range of angles ever since. Although a great number of studies on morphological competition addressed competition in derivation, research has also provided evidence of its existence in inflection (i.e., *overabundance*, Thornton 2012).

Despite the duration may be variable, competition is expected to be resolved either by the obsolescence of (the sense in) one of the forms or by specialization. Such specialization can be semantic, by register or dialectal. Nevertheless, two or more forms may be in competition for a time until resolution takes place. Although the outcomes described for competition operate both in inflection and derivation, they may occur to a greater or lesser extent. Therefore, it must be highlighted that there also exist differences between both categories and, thus, competition must be addressed separately in each domain.

Regarding derivation, competition has been generally understood as the co-existence of two or more patterns that express the same meaning. The main aim of the research considering competition in this sense has been the identification of the restrictions that guide the selection of one or the other pattern. However, from a more restrictive perspective, competitors are expected to be not only synonyms but also to be derived from the same base and be distributed in the same way (Fradin 2019). While research into competition has often focused on the first type, some studies have described how competition is resolved in competing doublets. As Romaine argues (2004: 1638):

> It is particularly instructive to compare word formation processes which compete for the same bases. In such cases the factors constraining productivity become clearer, and it is evident that synchronic restrictions on productivity are essentially the result of diachronic changes.

Competition has been researched for both prefixation and suffixation and in nominal, adjectival and verbal derivation. Concerning the latter, the influence of restrictions guiding the preference for one or the other affix is in some cases still unclear. Furthermore, both the restrictions and the affixes considered vary from author to author: while Schneider (1987) assesses the weight of phonological, morphological and semantic restrictions as well as extra-linguistic factors in the selection of *-en*, *-ify* and *-ize* suffixation, Kjellmer (2001) also considers the role of the frequency of the base in *be-*, *en-*, *-ate*, *-en*, *-ify* and *-ize* affixation, but leaves conversion aside; Plag (1999) concludes that both phonological and semantic restrictions are at play in the competition of the verbalizing affixes and conversion, at least in 20th century English, and Gottfurcht (2008) concludes that verbal derivation is also influenced by the *Semantic Category Distribution Effect*. Although both Plag (1999) and Gottfurcht (2008) include verbal doublets, there is no reference to the outcomes of such competition. More specific research into verbal doublets in *-ize* suffixation and conversion (Fernández-Alcaina 2017) has illustrated the various ways in which competition can be resolved. In some cases, the information provided by the members of the paradigms of these verbs can also cast light on the resolution of competition in less clear cases (Fernández-Alcaina & Čermák 2018). These conclusions, however, need to be tested in other pairs of competitors and other semantic categories.

Chapter 2: Method

2.1 Introduction

The study of morphological competition has benefited from the use of online versions of historical dictionaries and from the data available by use of electronic corpora. In the last decades, some empirical studies on competition have also made use of the Internet as a corpus. This chapter describes the resources available for the study of competition and the method used for both the extraction and analysis of the patterns competing for the formation of English verbs and of their derivational paradigms.

2.2 The *Oxford English Dictionary* and competition

The *Oxford English Dictionary* (henceforth, OED) is a historical dictionary containing around 600,000 words and currently under revision on a quarterly basis. Despite the fact that the use of dictionaries may bias the study of competition due to their limited coverage of neologisms, the OED, unlike learner or desk dictionaries, offers a comprehensive coverage of low frequency words in English. In fact, a test for the inclusion of low-frequency *-ness* and *-ize* words carried out by Plag (1999) based on data from the OED and the COBUILD corpus shows that 'the number of neologisms in the OED can reliably be used to tell productive processes from unproductive ones', i.e., available from unavailable processes (Plag 1999: 99). In the case of *-ize* verbs, the coverage of neologisms is even greater if compared to the coverage of nouns in *-ness*. This suggests that new verbs are more easily noticeable than new nouns possibly because the number of verbs is lower than that of nouns. Therefore, whereas lexicographic data may be a good index of what is available and what is not, the number of attestations of each word cannot be taken as an index of frequency and, thus, profitability cannot be measured based on lexicographic data (Plag 1999).

As a historical dictionary, the OED contains information regarding the etymology of the entries recorded. However, some entries do not show their precise etymological origins. Similarly, distinguishing borrowings from English coinages is not always without problems (see Nevalainen 1999: 397; Kaunisto 2009: 78).

Inconsistencies in the systematicity of the definitions provided by the OED are also noticed but, as the OED has gone under continuous revision since its first publication at the end of the 19th century, this is an unavoidable drawback. Several studies on competition make use of a series of keywords for the search of specific semantic categories, e.g., 'property' and 'state' for the extraction of abstract and STATIVE nouns (Arndt-Lappe 2014; Lara-Clares 2017, respectively), or 'cause' for the extraction of CAUSATIVE verbs (Fernández-Alcaina 2017). While the method is suitable for the extraction of a sample, it is important to keep in mind that entries belonging to the same category may be excluded, e.g., *Aladdinize* (Fernández-Alcaina & Čermák 2018).

Regarding use and distribution, the OED specifies whether entries are 'in use', 'rare', 'obsolete', 'dialectal' or belong to a specific register or domain. Some authors notice a literary bias in the quotations used in the first versions of the OED where texts were often chosen according to literary prestige (Nevalainen 1999: 337). However, technological progress has allowed the inclusion of other text sources such as television scripts.[10]

What makes the OED particularly interesting for the study of competition is the information about the lifespan of the entries. Various studies on morphological competition rely on the earliest and latest attestation dates to compare the availability and unavailability of competitors (Anshen & Aronoff 1999; Bauer 2001; Kaunisto 2009; Bauer et al. 2010; Díaz-Negrillo 2017, among others). In any case, conclusions based on attestation dates must be considered with caution because the earliest attestation date of an entry does not necessarily reflect the earliest use of the word, but the first written record in the OED. Similarly, words may be used long after the latest attestation date recorded (Bauer 2006: 178).[11] Since the attestation dates provided by the OED rely on the availability of records, some entries are known to have gaps in their dates (Nevalainen 1999). Whether these gaps are a consequence of *renewed availability* (Bauer 2014), *reborrowing* (Nevalainen 1999: 337) or simply of the lack of records is a question that remains unanswered in most cases. For some authors, such as Allan (2012: 25), the absence of attestations for a period of time does not necessarily entail that the word is in disuse. Since gaps may alter the results obtained when researching the competition of two forms, they have been included in the analysis and representation of the competing verbs here (see Section 2.3.3 for details on how gaps are handled here).

Overall, the use of lexicographic data for the study of morphological competition has insurmountable drawbacks inherent to the very nature of dictionaries,

---

10 https://public.oed.com/history/rewriting-the-oed/collecting-the-evidence/ (accessed 2021-05-13).

11 Nevalainen (1999: 339) notices an imbalance of primary sources in the OED depending on the author.

e.g., incomplete information due to lacking or unclear records. Nonetheless, previous and ongoing research into competition has proved the validity of the OED data for the study of past competing processes and their availability, especially if this is combined with corpus data (Fernández-Alcaina 2017; Smith 2020).

It is also important to note that the OED is currently undergoing a major revision which involves the addition of new entries and subsenses and the amendment and updating of existing material (Simpson 2004). This includes the redating of quotations and the inclusion of new attestations (Allan 2012: 19) and the revision of the availability of a form for certain senses. These two aspects that are crucial for the study of the availability of coexisting forms as earliest and latest attestation dates are used here to draw the evolution of competition.

Let's illustrate the importance of distinguishing OED2 entries from OED3 with the cluster *savage/savagize*. As described in more detail in Section 3.4.1.1, both forms compete for a time for the sense 'make savage'. In OED2, both forms are unmarked regarding use, thus implying that the competition for the causative meaning is unresolved. The earliest and latest date of attestation of the sense 'render savage' for each entry are specified in (1) and (2):

(1) *savage*: render savage, barbarous, or fierce.
Dispositions not despicable, if they had not been ***sauaged*** *with a too carelesse rudenesse.*
[1611 Speed *Hist. Gt. Brit.* ix. viii. (1623) 563]

They are extremely good-natured and mild-tempered dogs, unless carefully ***'savaged'*** *by their masters.*
[1899 *Contemp. Rev.* Dec. 882]

(2) *savagize*: render savage or cruel
Earnshaw has been allowed to grow up on the farm, a man ***savageized****.*
[1848 *Tait's Mag.* XV. 140]

It was but natural that a man, who when he was close on middle-age had still his reputation and fortune to make [etc.],..should be soured and half ***savagised****.*
[1864 Gilfillan in *Mem.* (1892) 349]

The differences with OED3 are:

i) The sense 'make savage' in the converted verb is now tagged as 'obsolete'. The verb *savage* is however still available with the sense 'to attack verbally', which is not expressed by its competitor in *-ize*.

ii) The date of earliest and latest attestation for the verb *savagize* have changed (1794 and 2005, respectively) due to the inclusion of new material.

Since the study of the availability of competing processes largely relies on attestation dates, it is therefore essential to restrict the selection of entries to those updated in the OED3, in order to avoid misleading results about the profile and resolution of competition (see Section 2.3.2).

2.3 Corpora and competition

Corpora are another source of data for the study of competition. Among their advantages, corpus data allow the evaluation of the profitability of word-formation patterns by means of productivity measures proposed by Aronoff (1976), Baayen (2009) or Gaeta & Rica (2015), among others. However, it also presents disadvantages for the study of competition.

As pointed out by Kaunisto (2009: 85), results may be biased due to lack of data. Apart from corpus size, results may be biased by the variety of English represented or the span of time covered by the text samples, especially in diachronic research and, also in diachrony, by the uneven text type selection, for objective or subjective reasons.

Previous research into competition shows that the resolution of competition in the cluster *quiet*^{V}/*quieten* is influenced by the variety of English considered: while *quiet* is preferred in AmE, as it has a frequency of 0.39 in the *British National Corpus* (Davies 2004, henceforth, BNC) and 2.77 in the *Corpus of Contemporary American English* (Davies 2008–, henceforth, COCA), BrE speakers seem to prefer its competitor *quieten*, which is recorded in the BNC with a frequency of 1.64 and 0.06 in the COCA (Fernández-Alcaina & Čermák 2018: 88).

Another disadvantage of using corpora for data collection is the problems they present to collect converted forms. Previous corpus-driven research into competition has solved this problem either by excluding conversion (e.g., Kjellmer 2001) or by complementing data with lexicographic resources (Fernández-Domínguez 2017; Lara-Clares 2017; Lara-Clares & Thompson 2019).

Internet may be also a corpus for data analysis. Lindsay & Aronoff (2013) analyse the competition in the clusters *-ic*/*-ical* and *-ize*/*-ify* using the *Google Estimated Total Hits* (ETM). A series of considerations need to be made when using the *Google ETM*:

i) the results do not represent the number of occurrences of a given form but the number of websites where it appears, and

ii) the results may contain 'false positives' (Lindsay & Aronoff 2013: footnote 6), such as typos or examples of non-native speech.

Apart from Google hits, the *Google Books Ngram Viewer* offers a corpus based on 500 billion words from 1500 until 2008. Despite the fact that one of the aspects subject to criticism is the alleged literary bias in the texts collected (as most belong to fiction), Davies & Chapman (2016: 147) conclude that '[...] the variety of text-types will be taken care of by a sample that is large enough to catch that variety. And this is precisely what Google Books has done'. Another disadvantage is the impossibility of accessing the whole context where the forms appear. Therefore, frequency results can be used only tentatively, at least, for the study of competition (Fernández-Alcaina 2017; Smith 2020).

2.4 Verbal competitors

2.4.1 Data collection

Previous research into verbal competition has usually focused on pairs of rival forms (Bauer et al. 2010; Lindsay 2012; Fernández-Alcaina 2017). In particular, research into the competition between causative verbs in *-ize* and conversion (Fernández-Alcaina 2017) shows that forms derived with affixes other than *-ize* or by conversion may also be in competition. For that reason, and in order to collect a sample as inclusive as possible both as regards the form and the meaning, this work addresses verbal derivation including:

i) both conversion and the verbalizing affixes *be-*, *en-/em-*, *-ate*, *-en*, *-ify* and *-ize*, and
ii) all the semantic categories for which verbs are attested to compete (e.g., INSTRUMENT).

The verbalizing prefixes described in the literature and considered in this analysis are:

i) *be-*: attached to native nominal (e.g., *benight*), adjectival (e.g., *beguilty*) and verbal bases (e.g., *beset*), usually with the sense ORNATIVE, even if PRIVATIVE and CAUSATIVE senses have also been recorded (Bauer et al. 2013: 268). The prefix *be-* may also serve as an intensification of the action denoted by the verb (Quirk et al. 1985: 1546).
ii) *en-/em-*: attached to native and non-native, chiefly nominal bases denoting LOCATIVE/DIRECTIONAL (e.g., *encapsule*), ORNATIVE (e.g., *encolour*) or RESULTATIVE (e.g., *enchurch*) senses (Quirk et al. 1985: 1546; Plag 1999: 219;

Bauer et al. 2013: 268). It can also be combined with adjectival bases (e.g., *enable*) with the sense CAUSATIVE and with verbal bases (e.g., *encause*). Plag (1999) identifies *en-* prefixation as a non-productive process in 20th century English derivation, and draws the conclusion that new formations in *en-/em-* are based on analogy.

Other verbalizing prefixes such as *a-* (Quirk et al. 1985: 1546; Bauer et al. 2013: 268), *for-*, *in-* and *im-* (Bauer et al. 2013: 268) have been excluded, because they usually appear in lexicalized formations that may hinder the identification of competitors. According to Bauer et al. (2013: 268), the prefix *a-* has both native and non-native origins and the variety of the meanings it expresses is varied and usually non-transparent (e.g., *allay*) and the prefix *for-*, inherited from Old English, appears in lexicalized forms and its meaning is not always clear (e.g., *forgive*). The forms *in-/im-* are spelling variants of *en-/em-*, some of them lexicalized with a different meaning. Regarding the use of the verbs *insure/ensure*, the online dictionary *Lexico*[12] indicates that both forms overlap in meaning. While *insure* is preferred for the commercial sense 'provide insurance', *ensure* denotes the more general sense 'make certain to happen', although in AmE English the latter may be expressed also by the form *insure*, e.g., *bail is posted to insure that the defendant appears for trial.*

Regarding suffixation, the verbalizing suffixes considered in this analysis are listed below:

i) *-ate*: attached mostly to nominal bases (e.g., *amalgamate*), although it can also be found with adjectival bases (e.g., *authenticate*), especially in formations prior to the 20th century (Gussmann 1987), as well as with complex bases and bound roots (e.g., *migrate*), but not with compounds or phrases. As for phonological factors, *-ate* verbs usually attach to bases ending in a trochee and no stress shift is involved. It usually induces truncation in dactylic bases, both ending in a vowel (e.g., *cativity* > *cativate*) or in a consonant (e.g., *alluvium* > *alluviate*). The suffix *-ate* is traditionally considered as an 'indicator of verbhood' (Plank 1981: 214; cf. also Marchand 1969: 258; Plag 1999: 212) but *-ate* verbs may be the result of other non-affixational processes such as back-formation (e.g., *formate* < *formation*), conversion (e.g., *citrate*), back-derivation or clipping (e.g., *patriate* < *repatriate*), analogical formation (e.g., *active/activate*) or simply idiosyncratic forms (e.g., *dissonate*) (see Plag

12 https://www.lexico.com/en

1999: 206–210 for details). From a semantic point of view, *-ate* verbs most commonly express the semantic categories:

a) ORNATIVE (e.g., *mercurate*),
b) RESULTATIVE (e.g., *phosphate*), and
c) CAUSATIVE (e.g., *passivate*).

ii) *-en*: usually attached to adjectival bases, expressing the sense CAUSATIVE (e.g., *deafen*) or used intransitively (Quirk et al. 1985: 1557; Plag 1999: 219). It can attach both to native and non-native bases (Bauer et al. 2013: 610). Regarding phonology, *-en* is usually preceded by monosyllabic bases ending in an obstruent (Bauer et al. 2013: 193), specifically /d/ and /t/ (Marchand 1969: 272; Bauer & Huddleston 2002: 1714 in Bauer et al. 2010: 7). Competition between *-en* suffixation and conversion is well-attested in the literature (Quirk et al. 1985: 1562; Plag 1999: 219; Bauer et al. 2010).

iii) *-ify*: attached both to native and non-native nominal (e.g., *citify*), adjectival (e.g., *divinify*) and bound bases (e.g., *calcify*) and proper nouns (e.g., *Christify*). Regarding phonological restrictions, *-ify* suffixation usually applies in monosyllabic (e.g., *artify*) and iambic (e.g., *bourgeoisify*) bases that carry the stress on the syllable preceding the suffix (Plag 1999: 197). Stress-shift is not common. Whereas bases with final unstressed /i/ coalesce with the suffix, consonant-final deletion is not attested. Exceptions to these general constraints may give rise to doublets *-ize*/*-ify* (Plag 1999: 201; Bauer et al. 2013: 287). In semantic terms, *-ify* verbs can express a range of senses, most of them also occurring in *-ize* verbs (Plag 1999: 195; Bauer et al. 2013: 283):

a) INCHOATIVE (e.g., *acidify*),
b) CAUSATIVE (e.g., *diversify*),
c) RESULTATIVE (e.g., *yuppify*),
d) ORNATIVE (e.g., *youthify*),
e) LOCATIVE (e.g., *tubify*) and, to a lesser extent,
f) SIMILATIVE (e.g., *Lewisify*), and
g) PERFORMATIVE (e.g., *speechify*).[13]

iv) *-ize*: attached to native and non-native nominal and adjectival bases to form in both transitive and intransitive uses of the verb. Regarding phonological restrictions, *-ize* suffixation applies in usually attached to trochaic bases (e.g., *randomize*, *dandyize*) and dactylic bases ending in a consonant (e.g.,

13 *-ify* suffixation is commonly used with neoclassical bases. Other types of bases are often facetious or pejorative (e.g., *speechify*, *dandify*) (Quirk et al. 1985: 1557).

hospitalize), and where the final vowel is deleted (e.g., *memorize*). Non-dactylic vowel-final bases that remain intact are also possible (e.g., *ghettoize*). Haplology also occurs in bases such as *feminine* (< *feminize*) in order to avoid identical 'adjacent syllables' (Plag 1999: 185). Stress shift is rare (Plag 1999: 171) (see Plag 1999 for a detailed account of the phonological restrictions of *-ize* verbs). Some bases may make use of extenders (e.g., *mediocritize* < *mediocre*).[14] Verbs in *-ize* can express a range of semantic categories (Plag 1999: 125; Bauer et al. 2013: 287):[15]

a) LOCATIVE (e.g., *hospitalize*),
b) ORNATIVE (e.g., *accessorize*),
c) CAUSATIVE[16] (e.g., *randomize*),
d) RESULTATIVE (e.g., *crystallize*),
e) INCHOATIVE (e.g., *aerosolize*),
f) PERFORMATIVE (e.g., *philosophize*), and
g) SIMILATIVE (e.g., *Boswellize*).

Finally, conversion is usually considered the most productive verb-formation process (Plag 1999: 219; Kastovsky 2005: 36; Bauer et al. 2013: 277), perhaps due to the variety of base types it can take, as they can be 'simplex, derived, or compound nouns and adjectives, onomatopoeic expressions and phrases' as well as prepositions, adverbs,[17] interjections and conjunctions (Bauer et al. 2013: 278). Converted verbs are also semantically diverse. In fact, Plag (1999: 220) claims that '[…] there should be no specific meaning attached to the process of zero-derivation at all'. However, apart from idiosyncratic meanings, some converted verbs may fall into the categories described for affixational process (Bauer et al. 2013: 285):

---

14 Instead of extenders, another form where adjustment is not needed can be set as the base (e.g., *mediocrity* > *mediocritize*) (Bauer et al. 2013: 270).

15 As described in Plag (1999) for 20th century formations. Older formations may display other semantic categories not included in the list.

16 Traditionally, FACTITIVE is used to refer to deadjectival formations and CAUSATIVE to denominal ones. However, since the distinction may appear as doubtful in the description of derived verbs, CAUSATIVE is used as the cover term to refer to both categories (Rainer 1993: 235, 238 in Plag 1999: 195). Similarly, the distinction between CAUSATIVE and RESULTATIVE is often ambiguous and both can be merged into the category CAUSATIVE (Plag 1999: 132).

17 Now considered unproductive (Bauer et al. 2013: 278).

i) LOCATIVE (e.g., *archive*),
ii) ORNATIVE (e.g., *marmalade*),
iii) CAUSATIVE (e.g., *sober*),
iv) RESULTATIVE (e.g., *package*),
v) INCHOATIVE (e.g., *gel*),
vi) PERFORMATIVE (e.g., *tango*),
vii) SIMILATIVE (e.g., *chauffeur*),
viii) INSTRUMENT (e.g., *hammer*),
ix) PRIVATIVE (e.g., *bark*), and
x) STATIVE (e.g., *bay*).

2.4.2 Data source selection

Two types of resources were tested for the collection of competing verbs. Specifically, three test were carried out using both corpus and lexicographic resources.

The first test extracted data from the *British National Corpus Frequency List*, which contains 616,568 lemmas ordered by frequency and tagged for word-class and, within frequency, in alphabetical order. The main advantage of using a frequency list is that it gathers all the types found in the BNC and provides information regarding word-class and frequency. Data extraction from the list is easily done by using the software *Scáthach* (Lara-Clares & Lara-Clares 2016), which allows filtering results by word-class, word-size and affix. It also allows to remove strings containing numbers or punctuation marks such as hyphens, slashes or brackets.

An initial list containing 2,368 verbs ending in *-ate*, *-ize*, *-ify* and *-en* was extracted from the *BNC Frequency List*. As the pairing of potential competitors was done automatically based on formal identity, the list obtained needed manual checking in order to discard forms sharing a similar string of characters but not a common base (e.g., *beat* 'strike repeatedly' vs *beatify* 'pronounce a person to be in enjoyment of heavenly bliss'). The final list obtained contains 68 pairs of competitors.

In a second test, two frequency lists containing suffixed verbs were extracted from two diachronic corpora, following the same procedure described for the first test:

i) The *Penn-Helsinki Parsed Corpus of Early Modern English* (Kroch et al. 2004, henceforth, PPCEME) is a syntactically annotated corpus that consists of c. 1.8 million words. It includes prose text samples dated between 1500 and 1710.

ii) The *Early English Book Online corpus* (henceforth, EEBO) is an annotated corpus containing texts from the 1470s to the 1690s. It consists of 755 million words.[18]

In this case, only 13 pairs of verbs were identified as competitors. This may be partly a consequence of the restriction of the corpora to a specific period since instances of pairs where the members are first attested in different periods are not uncommon (e.g., *English* 1450–/*Englishize* 1799–).

In view of the low number of competitors extracted form corpora, in the third test, a list of suffixed and non-suffixed verbs was collected from the OED3. Since the dictionary is continually updated and in order to guarantee the comparability of the data, the extraction of competing forms is restricted to those forms updated in the OED3 (see Section 2.2). The information from the OED used in the data description of the competitors was gathered from November 2018 to February 2019.[19]

Entries are apparently updated in a stratified way. This has both advantages and disadvantages. On the one hand, some competitors where one of the forms appears to be frequent in use need to be excluded because the entry was not updated, e.g., the latest attestation date for the verb *lengthen* in the OED goes back to 1891, even though it is relatively frequent in Present-Day English. On the other hand, the fact that the updating process does not proceed in alphabetical order allows the collection of entries throughout the dictionary. Furthermore, morphologically related entries usually belong to the same OED version, and this makes the comparison of competitors and their derivatives easier.

Previous research (Fernández-Alcaina 2017) relies on a list of 816 verbs in *-ize* extracted from the OED filtered by affix (i.e., *-*ize*), word-class (i.e., verb), language of origin (i.e., English) and the keywords contained in the definitions used for the gloss of the semantic category CAUSATIVE (typically 'make', 'render', and 'cause'). Filtering the verbs by their language of origin may make identification of potential competitors and exclusion of borrowings easier. The first 20 entries of the list used in previous research were manually checked and compared with the first 20 verbal entries of a list where no filters were applied, in order to compare the type of entries excluded with those that were not. After comparison, verbs described as 'From a proper name, combined with an English

18 Accessed via https://www.korpus.cz/.

19 In the remaining of this book, OED always refers to the third version (OED3), unless specified.

element' (e.g., *Aladdinize*) were excluded, leaving out verbs with foreign bases but derived within English which are also, for this reason, of relevance here. In view of these problems, a list of 6,784 verbs was collected from the OED filtered by the suffixes *-ate*, *-ize*, *-ify* and *-en*.

Suffixed verbs were screened for potential converted competitors that share the same base (e.g., *powder/powderize*). A total of 264 groups of verbs were identified as involving instances of competition for, at least, one of their senses listed in the OED.

Although lexicographic resources also have drawbacks (e.g., biased information as a result of unsystematic lexicographic practice), they supply information about etymology, meaning and use, all essential for research on competition. The use of the OED also allows collection of competing forms across periods without the need for combining sources.

2.4.3 Data processing

Since competition is assessed at the level of the sense, several clusters may arise from the same pair of forms. Tab. 1 describes the template used for the analysis of competitors taking as example the competition between the verbs *powder* and *powderize*.

As specified below, sense 4a in the OED for *powder* ('apply cosmetic powder to skin') competes with sense 1 in the entry *powderize* ('= *powder* 4a'). Following the semantic classification provided by Bauer et al. (2013), the cluster is classified here as ORNATIVE.

Another cluster, classified as RESULTATIVE, is formed by the senses 8a in *powder* ('reduce to powder') and sense 2 in *powderize* ('reduce to powder'). In all the cases mentioned, the verb has a transitive use.

The template used also contains information regarding the number of senses of each entry in the OED as well as their status, i.e., in use, obsolete, rare, archaic, dialectal or belonging to a particular register or domain. Whether the sense in competition is tagged with any of these labels is specified in the template (in the column 'Status'), which allows for a classification of the clusters as displaying resolved or unresolved competition. Based on the clusters describe in Tab. 1, the cluster *powder*^{4a}/*powderize*^{1} is an example of resolved competition, since only the converted form is available at present, while its competitor in *-ize* is tagged as 'obsolete'. In contrast, the resultative cluster *powder*^{8a}/*powderize*^{2} is an example of unresolved competition, as both senses are apparently available in Present-Day English.

The dates of earliest and latest attestation for each of the senses in competition are also included as they allow for the representation of the development of competition (see Fig. 1).

Tab. 1. A template for the description of competing verbs based on the information provided by the OED and semantically classified

Lemma	**Sense**	**Meaning**			**Senses**						**Status**	**Timeline**	
		Semantic category	**Definition**	**Trans./ Intr.**	**In use**	**Obs./ Rare**	**Arch.**	**Dial.**	**Reg./ Dom.**	**Total**		*	†
powder	4a	ORNATIVE	apply cosmetic to skin	trans.	6	4	0	0	0	10	in use	1616	2002
powderize	1		= *powder* 4a	trans.	1	1	0	0	0	2	obsolete	1800	1800
powder	8a	RESULTATIVE	reduce to powder	trans.	6	4	0	0	0	10	in use	1400	1991
powderize	2		reduce to powder	trans.	1	1	0	0	0	2	in use	1903	1998

Apart from the information included in Tab. 1, the number of quotations provided by the OED for each sense has been also taken into account. This does not mean that it is considered as an indicator of frequency, but rather that it is a way of telling entries with restricted use from those that seem to be more common. Specifically, quotations have been considered for:

i) once-attested forms (e.g., *peacockize*)
To go ietting idly or loytring vp and downe peacockising and courting of himselfe.
[1598, J. Florio, *Worlde of Wordes*]

ii) unique forms attested only in works by the same author (e.g., *nighen*)
Ympne to alle his halwen…to folk that neiȝneth to hym.
[a1400 *Prymer* (St. John's Cambr.) (1891) 26]
Streyne thow here chekes that neyȝneth nouȝt to the.
[a1400 *Prymer* (St. John's Cambr.) (1891) 53]

iii) forms attested as dictionary entries (e.g., *paroxytonize*)
Paroxytonize, to accent on the penultimate syllable.
[1904, N.E.D.]

Although the number of quotations recorded in the OED must not be taken as an indicator of their productivity, cases in which forms are attested once have been considered as they may indicate that creative innovations (Allan 2012). Similarly, quotations are also noted if they all belong to the same author (e.g., *blithen* 'make blithe' in Galt 1824, 1830 in the OED).

For the semantic classification of clusters, the categories used are those described for verbs by Bauer et al. (2013: 282–286) and listed below:

i) CAUSATIVE (e.g., *befoul, enlarge, passivate, deafen, diversify, randomize, sober*)
ii) INCHOATIVE (e.g., *acidify, aerosolize, gel*)
iii) INSTRUMENT (e.g., *hammer*)
iv) LOCATIVE (e.g., *encapsulate, tubify, hospitalize, archive*)
v) ORNATIVE (e.g., *beblood, enhat, mercurate, youthify, accessorize, marmalade*)
vi) PERFORMATIVE (e.g., *speechify, Boswellize, tango*)
vii) PRIVATIVE (e.g., *behead, bank*)
viii) RESULTATIVE (e.g., *enchurch, phosphate, yuppify, crystallize, package*)
ix) SIMILATIVE (e.g., *Lewisify, chauffeur*)
x) STATIVE (e.g., *bay*)

The timelines for the competitors under analysis were built using the OED earliest and latest attestation dates for each verb, and represented according to the chart model in Fig. 1:

i) The *x* axis specifies the years, from 500 to 2000. The years 500 and 800, which are OED Early Old English (henceforth, eOE) and Old English (henceforth, OE) attestations, are convenient labels for easier data comparison.
ii) The *y* axis specifies the base of the competing verbs within a cluster (e.g., *legend*[N]).
iii) The lines represent competing derived forms. In the example shown in Fig. 1, the broken line stands for *-ize* derivatives (e.g., *legendize*) and the solid line stands for converted verbs (e.g., *legend*[V]).

Whenever there is a gap in the attestation dates cited in the OED, the gap has been noted and represented in the timeline chart (see Fig. 1). For example, for the base *mongrel*, a converted verb (in black) and a suffixed verb in *-ize* (in grey) are earliest attested at the beginning of the 17th century. However, while the OED provides evidence on the continuity of the availability of the suffixed verb, there is a gap in the attestation dates for the converted verb between the end of the 17th century and the mid-20th century.

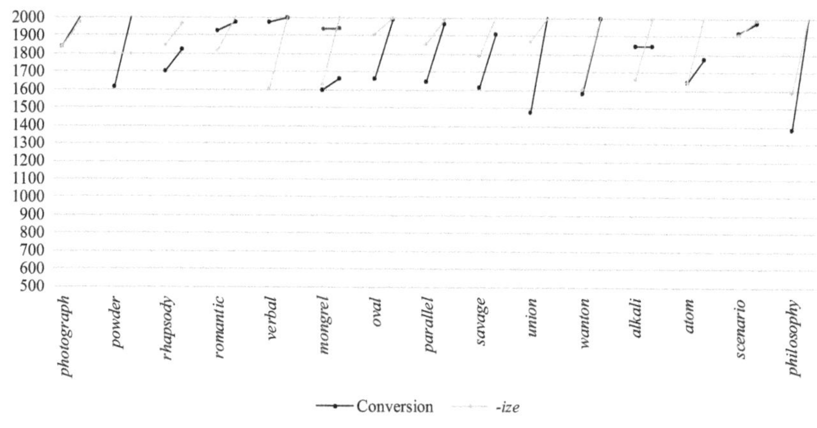

Fig. 1. Timeline chart model for the historical development of verbal competing bases. The black line stands for conversion; the grey line, for *-ize* suffixation

Additional data from corpora and contemporary dictionaries have been considered to complement the information provided by the OED for the study of competition in verbs. Specifically, the resources used are:

i) two historical corpora:
   a) *English Historical Book Collection* (henceforth, EHBC),[20] is a corpus collection containing texts dated between 1472 and 1820 from three corpora: EEBO (Phase I), *Eighteenth Century Collections Online* (ECCO) and Readex's Evans. The collection has a size of 826,296,048 words (987,242,247 tokens). The collection has been used for the study of diachronic competition of adjectival doublets (Smith 2020).
   b) *Corpus of Historical American English* (Davies 2010, henceforth, COHA), containing more than 475 million words from texts between 1820s and 2010s and well-balanced by genre and decade.
ii) two contemporary corpora:
   a) COCA, containing more than one million words from texts dated from 1990 to 2019 and well-balanced as regards genre.
   b) *iWeb: The 14 Billion Web Corpus* (Davies 2018, henceforth, iWeb) contains 14 billion words from 22 million websites.
iii) the derivational paradigms where the competitors are allocated, in order to check whether the mapping of a particular sense onto the derivative can shed light on the prevalence of a form over its competitor.

Whenever required, contemporary dictionaries (*Collins* and *Merriam-Webster*) have also been used as complementary information regarding the definition and the status of the competitors analysed, especially for those attested to be in use in Present-Day English.

2.5 Paradigm construction

2.5.1 Data collection

The data collection method used for the construction of paradigms is partly based on Fernández-Alcaina & Čermák (2018) for the competition between conversion and *-ize* suffixation. In previous research, derivatives were extracted both from the OED and the COCA. This was in order to collect as many derived forms

20 Accessed via *Sketch Engine* (https://www.sketchengine.eu/) (accessed 2021-04-07).

as possible. However, as this study is wider in scope than the above reference and focuses on verbal affixation rather than on two specific processes, it collects potential members of the verbal subparadigms exclusively from the OED.

In accordance with an inclusive approach, data collection for the construction of paradigms considers:

i) available and unavailable derived forms in the creation of the subparadigms, and
ii) forms derived by combining forms and affixoids. In view of the difficulty to separate combining forms and affixoids from compounding (not considered here), only the combining forms and affixoids classified as such in Quirk et al. (1985), Stockwell & Minkova (2009) and Bauer et al. (2013) are considered. Tab. 2 shows the list of combining forms and affixoids classified according to their position:

Tab. 2. Combining forms and affixoids used for data selection based on Quirk et al. (1985), Stockwell & Minkova (2009) and Bauer et al. (2013)

Initial position						**Final position**
anti-	*micro-*	*non-*	*proto-*	*semi-*		*-like*
demi-	*mid-*	*post-*	*pseudo-*	*sub-*	*ultra-*	*-some*
hyper-	*multi-*	*pre-*	*quasi-*	*super-*	*under-*	*-wise*
mega-	*nano-*	*pro-*	*re-*	*supra-*		

For the identification of derivatives in the OED, forms were searched for using the expression **lemma** (e.g., **tender**),[21] resulting in a list containing a high number of derivatives from a particular base. The lists were then analysed to exclude irrelevant cases of accidental formal identity (e.g., *pretender* < *pretend* 'a person who makes a profession or assertion, esp. falsely or hypocritically') and compounds (e.g., *tender-foreheaded* 'modest, meek').

2.5.2 Data processing

The data obtained were analysed following the template below. An example of the partial paradigm of the base *mongrel* ('the offspring or result of cross-breeding, miscreation, mixed married') is given in Tab. 3.

21 In some bases, such as *discipline*, the last grapheme is dropped as it is one of the requirements for suffixes to attach (e.g., *disciplinable*, *disciplinize*).

Information regarding the word-class of the forms, the earliest and latest attestation dates and the definition is according to the OED.

In the case of this subparadigm, the verbs *mongrel* and *mongrelize* began to compete around 1630 (when the form in *-ize* is first attested), but in the second half of the 17th century, the converted form was lost and only the *-ize* verb remained. The preference for the *-ize* verb is supported by further derivation in *-ation* (*mongrelization*), *-ing* (*mongrelizing*^{N}) and *-ed* (*mongrelized*):[22]

mongrel	*mongrel*^{V}	1602	1662	make mongrel				
	mongrelize^{V}	1629	–	make mongrel	*mongrelized*^{ADJ}	1857	–	made mongrel
					mongrelization^{N}	1868	–	action of making mongrel
					mongrelizing^{N}	1922	–	action of making mongrel

2.6 Summary

This chapter summarizes the method used for the collection and analysis of competition in verbal clusters. The use of the OED3 for the study of diachronic competition presents a series of advantages over corpora, e.g., identification of a higher number of competing forms, attestation dates and information regarding status and use. However, it also presents disadvantages that are inherent to its very nature, such as the lack of available records or inconsistencies in the structure of the definitions provided, which may hinder the identification of competitors.

Since the study of past competition and its resolution inevitably relies on the attestation dates provided by the dictionary, the clusters analysed in this book are restricted to those forms that have been updated in the third version of the OED. Otherwise, the inclusion of data from the OED2 could lead to misleading results of competition in respect of attestation dates and status.

Despite the OED has proved to be a powerful tool for the study of competition regarding both data collection and data processing, a more detailed analysis of the phenomenon requires the combination of different sources. Specifically, for this piece of research, lexicographic information has been complemented with historical (EHBC and COHA) and contemporary (COCA, iWeb) corpora, as

22 In order to follow the most inclusive approach possible, the suffixes *-ed* and *-ing* are included whenever they are recorded in the OED as separate entries, either as adjectives (in *-ed* or *-ing*) or as nouns (in *-ing*), despite their controversial nature as intermediate cases on the inflection/derivation cline.

well as with synchronic dictionaries (*Collins* and *Merriam-Webster*). Besides, based on previous research (Fernández-Alcaina & Čermák 2018), the study of competition considering the paradigms where the competing forms are allocated may also shed light on the direction in the resolution of competition.

Chapter 3: General remarks on the competition in verbal formation

3.1 Introduction

The study of the competition in verbalizing affixes lends itself to a wealth of further descriptive results. This chapter addresses the competing patterns identified in the sample and provides an outline of the most relevant aspects of the profile of competition and its resolution in verbal formation.[23]

A total of 264 groups of verbs in which forms compete at least for one sense were identified in the sample. Specifically:

i) 200 groups of denominal verbs (e.g., *pressure/pressurize*),
ii) 63 groups of deadjectival verbs (e.g., *savage/savagize*), and
iii) one group of deadverbial verbs (i.e., *nigh/nighen*).

The remaining of the chapter focuses on the competition in denominal and deadjectival clusters, since the low number of deadverbial verbs does not allow for a comparison of the profile of competition displayed. Specifically, an overview of the competition displayed by the clusters analysed in this book is provided in Section 3.2. Section 3.3 elaborates on the polysemy of the patterns in competition and the various degrees of synonymy identified. Sections 3.4 and 3.5 describe in detail the competition in denominal and deadjectival formation, respectively. Section 3.6 addresses the resolution of competition regarding the outcomes (i.e., whether resolved, past or ongoing), the time it takes and the direction in which competition is resolved as well as the profile of the form that remains in use (i.e., earliest vs latest attested form). Section 3.7 discusses the implications of the results obtained. The chapter closes with a summary in Section 3.8.

3.2 Overview

This section introduces the general profile displayed by the clusters in the sample regarding competing patterns in terms of their meaning and the resolution of the competition they are involved in.

23 The y-axis of the charts presented in this chapter has been set to 50, 250, 500 or 2000. Scale values are specified for each chart.

A total of 264 groups of verbal competitors were extracted from the OED.[24] Specifically:

i) 236 groups were pairs of competitors, and
ii) 28 groups contain three or more competing forms.

The number of groups of competitors in which each of the verbalizing patterns considered here is represented (in percentages) in Fig. 2:

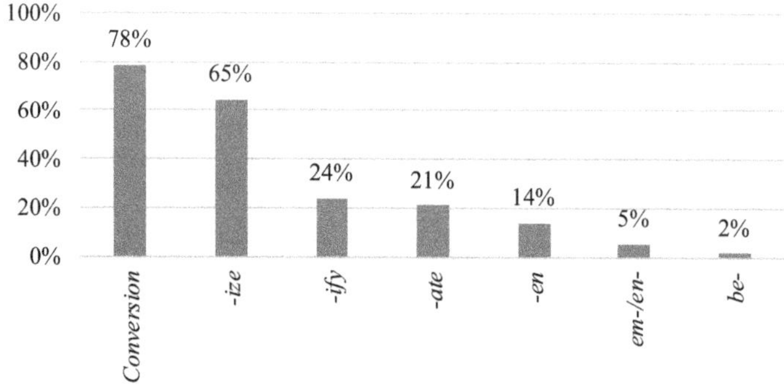

Fig. 2. Competing patterns in clusters

Conversion appears as the most common process in competition: of the 264 clusters where competition is attested, 78 % (i.e., 208 clusters) have a converted verb as one of the competitors, while affixation is a secondary competitor, with the following affixes in decreasing order of frequency:

i) Groups where one of the forms is a suffixed verb in *-ize* amount to 65 % of the clusters, i.e., 171 clusters.
ii) Groups where one of the forms is a suffixed verb in *-ify* amount to 24 % of the clusters, i.e., 63 clusters.
iii) Groups where one of the forms is a suffixed verb in *-ate* amount to 21 % of the clusters, i.e., 55 of the clusters.
iv) Groups where one of the competitors is a suffixed verb in *-en* amount to 14 % of the clusters, i.e., 37 clusters.

24 Unless otherwise specified, 'OED' in the remaining of the chapter refers to OED3.

Affixation by a verbalizing prefix is marginal, as the number of groups in which one of the competitors is derived by means of prefixation is considerably lower (i.e., 18 clusters in total). Specifically:

i) Groups where one of the forms is a prefixed verb in *em-/en-* amount to 5 % of the clusters, i.e., 14 clusters.
ii) Groups where one of the forms is a prefixed verb in *be-* amount to 2 % of the clusters, i.e., four clusters.

Tabs. 3 and 4 show the combinations of competing patterns identified ordered by their frequency in the sample:

Tab. 3. Competing doublets

Pattern	%	Groups	Example
Ø vs *-ize*	42 %	100	*mongrel/mongrelize*
Ø vs *-en*	14 %	34	*pink/pinken*
-ify vs *-ize*	10 %	24	*alkalify/alkalize*
Ø vs *-ify*	10 %	24	*palsy/palsify*
-ate vs *-ize*	9 %	20	*objectivate/objectivize*
Ø vs *-ate*	8 %	18	*petition/petitionate*
Ø vs *em-/en-*	5 %	12	*power/empower*
Ø vs *be-*	2 %	4	*lord/belord*

Tab. 4. Competing triplets (or above)

Pattern	%	Groups	Example
Ø vs *-ate* vs *-ize*	39 %	11	*carbon/carbonate/carbonize*
Ø vs *-ify* vs *-ize*	29 %	8	*immune/immuniy/immunize*
-ate vs *-ify* vs *-ize*	11 %	3	*personate/personify/personize*
Ø vs *-en* vs *-ify*	7 %	2	*neat/neaten/neatify*
Ø vs *en-* vs *-ize*	7 %	2	*empatron/patron/patronize*
Ø vs *-en* vs *-ize*	3 %	1	*quiet/quieten/quietize*
Ø vs *-ate* vs *-ify* vs *-ize*	3 %	1	*fossil/fossilate/fossilify/fossilize*

The data above refer to the pairs or groups of verbs where competition occurs without distinguishing those clusters in which competition is present in more than one sense. However, as argued in Section 2.3.2 and already pointed in previous research into competition (cf. Díaz-Negrillo 2017; Fernández-Alcaina

2017; Lara-Clares 2017; Fernández-Alcaina & Čermák 2018, Lara-Clares & Thompson 2019; Smith 2020), any account of competition must necessarily be done at the level of the sense, thus allowing for the distinction of several clusters for the same pair of forms, which may differ in the semantic category they express and the stage of resolution they display. Specifically, a total of 350 clusters were identified after semantic classification. Based on the number of competitors they contain:

i) 319 clusters are doublets,
ii) 30 clusters are triplets, and
iii) only one cluster contains more than three competitors (*fossil/fossilate/fossilify/fossilize*).

As regards the word-class of the base, 248 clusters are denominal, 101 clusters are denominal and only one cluster is deadjectival. The next section elaborates on the polysemy of the patterns in competition and the various degrees of synonymy displayed by the clusters in the sample.

3.3 Polysemy and synonymy of competing verbs

3.3.1 Monosemy vs polysemy in competition

The number of groups of forms where competition is attested in at least one sense is 264, although competition between two or three monosemous verbs is attested only in 36 of them, i.e., 14 %. This is illustrated by the doublet *mongrel/mongrelize* ('make mongrel in breed, ethnic type, composition, character, etc.'), where the converted verb is marked as 'rare' in the OED (Tab. 5):

Tab. 5. An example of competition between monosemous forms

Lemma	Definition	Status	*	†
mongrel	= *mongrelize*	rare	1602	1662/1941[a]
mongrelize	make mongrel in breed	in use	1629	1991

[a]This example also illustrates cases where there is a gap in the earliest and latest attestation date of each competitor provided by the dictionary (see Chapter 2, Section 2.3.2).

In the remaining 228 groups of verbal competitors, at least one of the verbs has two or more senses (e.g., *objectify/objectize* 'make into an object') or both forms have more than one sense (e.g., *mission/missionize* 'conduct a religious mission'). Fig. 3 shows denominal and deadjectival clusters classified according to whether competition occurs between monosemous forms (Mon.), between a polysemous and a monosemous form (Pol. vs Mon.) or between polysemous forms (Pol. vs Pol.):

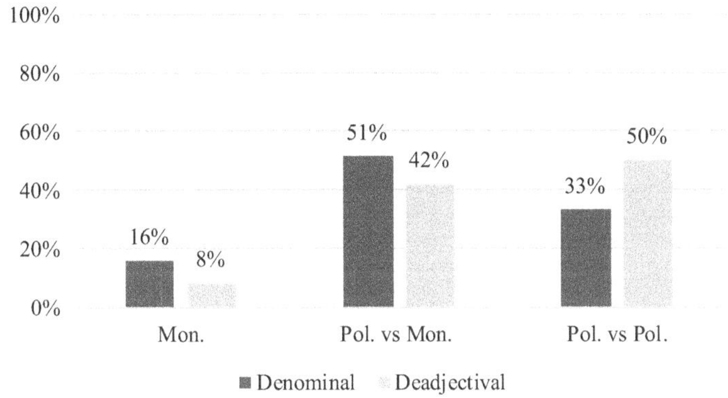

Fig. 3. Monosemy (mon.) and polysemy (pol.) in denominal (dark grey) and deadjectival (light grey) verbs

As shown in Fig. 3, competition between monosemous verbs occurs in 16 % of denominal clusters and 8 % of deadjectival verbs. The most common type of competition in denominal clusters is that between a polysemous form and a monosemous verb (i.e., 51 %), while the competition between two or more polysemous denominal verbs amounts to 42 %. Opposite results are found for deadjectival verbs, in which the competition between a polysemous and monosemous form is observed in 33 % of the clusters. Competition between two or more polysemous verbs is attested in 50 % of deadjectival clusters. The various degrees of synonymy displayed by the clusters identified are described in more detailed in Section 3.3.2.

3.3.2 Degrees of synonymy in clusters

3.3.2.1 One-to-one sense competition

Apart from clusters formed by monosemous verbs, as in the example of *mongrel/mongrelize* above, competition may be attested in only one of the senses of a polysemous verb. For example, in the cluster *savage/savagize*, the verbs competed for some time for the expression of the meaning 'make savage' (CAUSATIVE), as illustrated in Tab. 6:

Tab. 6. An example of competition only in one sense

Lemma	S	Semantics	Definition	Senses	Status	*	†
savage	2	CAUSATIVE	make savage	3	rare	1611	1910
savagize	-		make savage	1	in use	1794	2005

Notably, the converted verb *savage* has two more senses for which no competitor is attested in the OED:

(3) *savage*[25] 1. (intr.) To act in a savage manner; to be cruel or barbarous. *Obsolete.*

3. a. (trans.) To attack verbally.
b. (trans.) Of an animal or person: to attack ferociously.
c. (trans.) More generally: to damage or harm; to treat savagely.

The second (or third) attested form may not be necessarily a monosemous verb, as is the case of *savagize* ('make savage', cf. Tab. 6). In clusters where all the forms are polysemous, competition may still be restricted to one sense, e.g., *history/historify/historize* (Tab. 7):

Tab. 7. An example of competition between polysemous verbs

Lemma	S	Semantics	Definition	Sense classification			*	†
				In use	Obs./ Rare	Total		
historify	1		relate the history of	1	1	2	1586	1986
historize	1	PERFORMATIVE	relate the history of	2	1	3	1572	1995
history	1		write the history of	1	1	2	1475	2001

25 Sense numbering as in the OED.

3.3.2.2 Many-to-many sense competition

Competition may also occur between various senses, resulting in the intertwining of the senses of both competitors. In these cases, the same group of competing forms may lead to the distinction of various clusters according to the semantic category for which the forms compete. This can occur to several degrees: from clusters where competition is attested in two senses (e.g., the forms in the cluster *ripe*/*ripen* compete for both a causative and an inchoative meaning), to those where overlaps in meaning occur in all the senses listed in the dictionary, e.g., *character*/*characterize* (Tab. 8).

For the competition between the verbs *character*/*characterize*, five clusters have been identified according to their semantic category (Tab. 8):

Tab. 8. An example of competition between various senses

	Lemma	S	Semantic category	Sense classification			*	†
				In use	Obs./ Rare	Status		
1	*character*	2	ORNATIVE	2	3	obsolete	1555	1831
	characterize	2		3	2	rare	1594	2004
2	*character*	1	INSTRUMENT	2	3	literary	1555	1963
	character	3		2	3	rare	1589	1928
	characterize	1		3	2	obsolete	1581	1886
3	*character*	4	PERFORMATIVE	2	3	obsolete	1618	2008
	characterize	4		3	2	in use	1610	2010
4	*character*	5a	ORNATIVE	2	3	in use	1621	2006
	characterize	5		3	2	in use	1786	2009
5	*character*	5b	STATIVE	2	3	in use	1621	2006
	characterize	3		3	2	in use	1602	2010

In the first cluster, the converted verb is latest attested in the first half of the 19th century and marked as 'obsolete', whereas the latest attestation for the *-ize* competitor is 2004. The suffix *-ize* prevails over conversion for the expression of ORNATIVE, but the form is marked as 'now somewhat rare':

(4a) *character* 2. To represent, symbolize, portray; to be a representative or symbol of. *Obsolete.*

(4b) *characterize* 2. To represent, symbolize, portray. Now somewhat *rare.*

In the second cluster, competition for the expression of the category INSTRUMENT is attested between senses 1 and 3 of *character* and sense 1 in *characterize*. Specifically, the OED defines them as follows:

(5a)	*character*	1. To distinguish by particular marks, signs, or features; to stamp, mark. Now *literary*.
		3. To engrave, imprint, inscribe, or write on a surface. Frequently figurative and in figurative contexts. Now *somewhat rare*.
(5b)	*characterize*	1. To engrave, imprint, inscribe, or write (words, symbols, etc.) on or in something; to engrave, imprint, or inscribe (a surface, material, etc.) with something; also figurative and in figurative contexts. Also: to define in form or outline. *Obsolete*.

In the PERFORMATIVE cluster, competition seems to be resolved in favor of the *-ize* form, while the converted form is marked as 'obsolete' in the OED:[26]

(6a)	*character*	4. To describe the distinctive nature, features, or qualities.
(6b)	*characterize*	4. To describe the distinctive nature or features of; to specify the identifying qualities of, classify.

For clusters 4 and 5 (denoting the senses ORNATIVE and STATIVE), there does not seem to be a clear bias towards any of the forms at the time. For this reason, this type of clusters has been classified as 'ongoing competition':

(7a)	*character*	5a. To invest with a character, impart character to; usually in *passive*.
(7b)	*characterize*	5. To impart character to. †Also intransitive with object understood. In some cases difficult to distinguish from sense 3.
(8a)	*character*	5b. Of a feature or quality: to be typical or characteristic of.

26 Although the latest attestation date is 2008, dates preceding it refer back to the 19th century, the latest being from 1911.

(8b) *characterize* 3. Of a feature or quality: to define the character or identity of, to mark, distinguish; to be typical or characteristic of. †Also with complement.

As illustrated by the verbs *character*/*characterize*, clusters may not only differ in the categories for which the forms compete, but they may also evidence various stages in the resolution of competition. Thus, while the competition for the category PERFORMATIVE is resolved in favor of *-ize* suffixation, the two verbs remain in competition for the expression of the categories ORNATIVE and STATIVE.

3.4 Denominal clusters

Of the 350 clusters collected in the sample, 248 clusters are cases of competition between denominal verbs. Despite the fact that all the processes considered for the data collection are represented by at least one cluster, conversion and *-ize* suffixation are present in most of the patterns identified. Conversion appears as the most common process in competition in denominal verb formation (206 clusters) (Fig. 4). This may be explained on the basis of its uneven distribution across semantic categories as it is the only process that is found in all the semantic categories identified, even if some semantic categories are more common than others. Conversion is followed by the second most productive process in verb formation in English, i.e., *-ize* suffixation, which appears as one of the competing forms in 151 clusters:

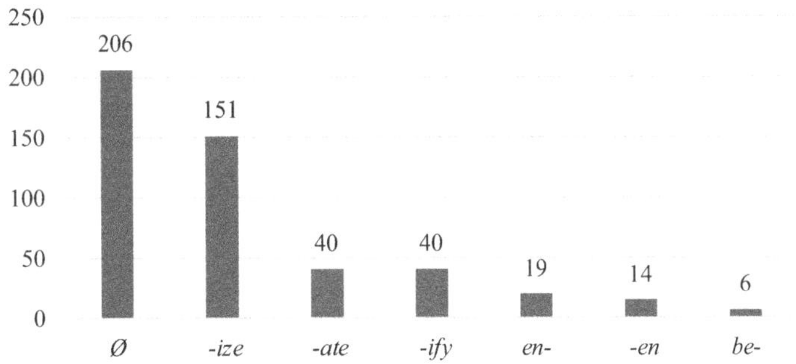

Fig. 4. Competing denominal processes

The rest of the processes identified in the sample are much less common: *-ate* and *-ify* suffixation are identified as competitors in 40 clusters each, *en-* prefixation is found in 19 clusters and *-en* prefixation in 14 clusters. Only six clusters contain a *be-* prefixed verb. The results obtained regarding the distribution of the processes in competition imply that the competition in denominal verb formation is mostly restricted to the competition of the two patterns identified as the most productive processes in English for verb formation, as argued by Plag (1999), i.e., conversion and *-ize* suffixation in denominal formation (e.g., *photograph/photographize* 'take a photograph').

Regarding the semantic categories for which competition in denominal verbal formation is attested, the distribution is uneven. However, the categories RESULTATIVE and ORNATIVE are the categories in which more competition is attested, as it is shown in Fig. 5. In particular, the sum of the two categories amounts to 55 % of the clusters analysed. In contrast, other categories such as LOCATIVE or PRIVATIVE are hardly found.[27]

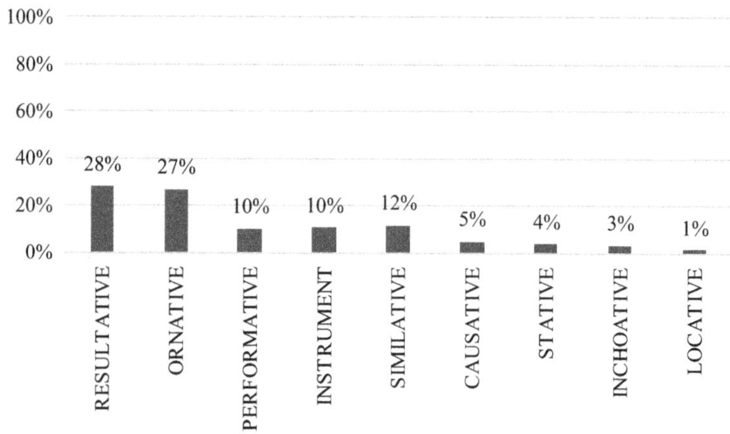

Fig. 5. Semantic categories for denominal clusters

The comparison of the semantic categories expressed by each pattern (Tab. 9) reveals that ORNATIVE is the only category expressed by all the patterns

27 The category PRIVATIVE is excluded from Fig. 5 as it is only represented by one cluster (i.e., > 1 %).

considered in this study, followed by RESULTATIVE. A converted competitor is found for all the semantic categories identified.

Tab. 9. Semantic categories in denominal clusters by pattern

	Conversion	*-ize*	*-ate*	*-ify*	*-en*	*en-*	*be-*
ORNATIVE	+	+	+	+	+	+	+
RESULTATIVE	+	+	+	+	+	+	
INSTRUMENT	+	+	+		+	+	
PERFORMATIVE	+	+	+	+			
SIMILATIVE	+	+	+	+		+	
CAUSATIVE	+	+	+	+			
INCHOATIVE	+	+	+	+	+		
STATIVE	+	+				+	+
LOCATIVE	+					+	
PRIVATIVE	+						

3.5 Deadjectival clusters

Competition among deadjectival verbs is identified in 101 of the 350 clusters in the sample. Fig. 6 shows the patterns identified according to the number of clusters in which they appear as competitors:

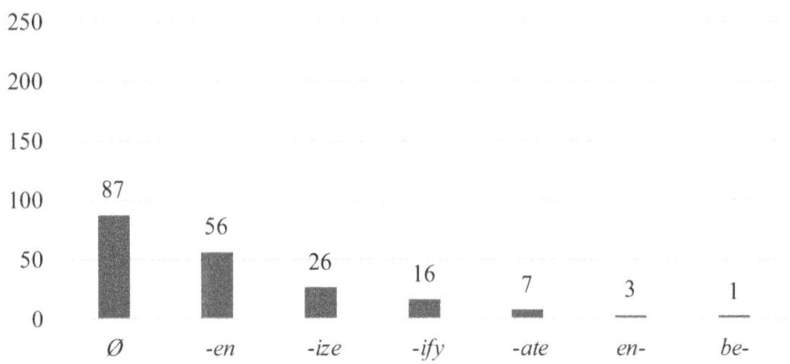

Fig. 6. Competing deadjectival processes

Conversion is also the most common process attested in the deadjectival clusters analysed, followed in this case by *-en* suffixation (e.g., *hard/harden* 'make hard'), which stands as the second most frequent process. In fact, as shown in Fig. 6, 54 % of the deadjectival clusters belong to the competition between conversion and *-en* suffixation. The rest of the pattern identified are represented by less than 15 % of the clusters.

Regarding semantic representation and in contrast to the uneven distribution of semantic categories in denominal formation, deadjectival competitors are mainly restricted to the expression of two categories: CAUSATIVE and INCHOATIVE, which amount to 90 % of the total number of deadjectival clusters (Fig. 7):

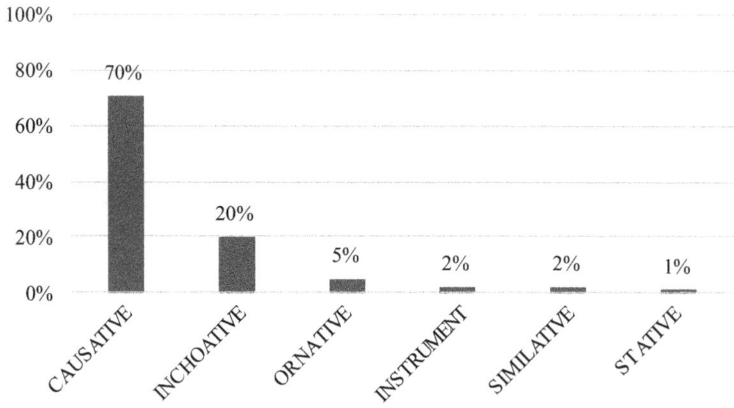

Fig. 7. Semantic categories for deadjectival clusters

As occurred in denominal formation, the comparison of the semantic categories expressed by each pattern shows that, while a converted competitor is identified for all the categories identified for deadjectival clusters, affixes show restrictions as regards semantics (Tab. 10):

Tab. 10. Semantic categories by pattern in deadjectival verb formation

	Conversion	*-ate*	*-en*	*-ify*	*-ize*	*be-*	*en-*
CAUSATIVE	+	+	+	+	+	+	+
INCHOATIVE	+		+	+	+		+
INSTRUMENT	+	+			+		
ORNATIVE	+		+	+	+		
SIMILATIVE	+				+		
STATIVE	+		+				

3.6 The resolution of competition

3.6.1 Outcomes of competition

According to the profile of competition, the clusters identified here have been classified as three groups:

i) Resolved competition, i.e., only one of the forms is attested to be in use in Present-Day English (e.g., *hazard/hazardize*†) (172 clusters).
ii) Past competition, i.e., all the forms are marked as in disuse by the OED (68 clusters, i.e., 19 %). The obsolescence of both forms may be explained either because they are replaced by a third form which does not share the same base (e.g., *perfection/perfectionate/perfectionize* 'bring to perfection') or simply because there is apparently no longer a need for that meaning to be expressed (e.g., *melancholy/melancholize* 'make melancholy').
iii) Ongoing competition, i.e., all the competitors in the cluster are unmarked regarding use in the OED (110 clusters, i.e., 32 %) (e.g., *adjective/adjectivize* 'turn into an adjective').

Fig. 8 shows the classification of denominal and deadjectival clusters depending on the profile of competition regarding resolution:[28]

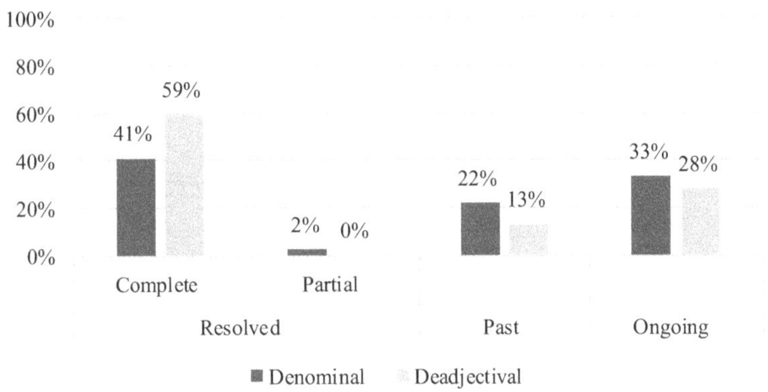

Fig. 8. Denominal and deadjectival clusteres classified by the profile of competition regarding resolution (i.e., resolved competition, past competition, ongoing competition)

28 Deadverbial verb formation is excluded from representation as there is only one cluster in the sample.

Most clusters in denominal and deadjectival verb formation are classified here as resolved competition. However, as shown in Fig. 8, nearly 60 % of deadjectival clusters display complete resolved competition, while the percentage of denominal clusters is 41 % for complete resolved competition and 2 % for partial resolved competition. Regarding past competition, the number of deadjectival clusters is considerably lower than the number of denominal clusters in which all the forms are no longer in use (13 % and 22 %, respectively). The number of denominal and deadjectival clusters in which competition is a priori unresolved is similar (33 % and 28 %, respectively). A more detailed analysis of each outcome of competition is provided in Sections 3.6.1.1–3.6.1.3.

3.6.1.1 Resolved competition

Of the 172 clusters classified as instances of resolved competition:

i) 166 clusters, i.e., 97 %, show resolved competition, insofar as only one of the forms remains in use (Tab. 11).

Tab. 11. An example of resolved competition in a triplet

Lemma	S	Semantic category	Definition	Status	*	†
statue2	2		turn a living being into a statue	rare	1628	1941
statuefy	2	RESULTATIVE	turn a living being into a statue	in use	1868	2006
statuize	-		make a statue of; turn into a statue	rare	1718	1944

ii) Six clusters, i.e., 3 %, show partial resolution. Partial resolution is here considered to occur whenever one of the members in a cluster with three or more forms has been ousted from competition (as attested by OED records), while the rest of the members are attested to continue in use. For example, in the cluster *pauperize/pauper/pauperate* 'make a pauper of', the form in *-ate* is marked as 'obsolete' by the OED, whereas the converted and the *-ize* verb are attested to be in use in the OED (Tab. 12).

Tab. 12. An example of partial resolution of competition

Lemma	Semantics	Definition	Status	*	†
pauperize		make a pauper of sb	in use	1834	1992
pauper	RESULTATIVE	= *pauperize*	in use	1841	2002
pauperate		= *pauperize*	obsolete	1839	1839

The outcomes of the resolution of competition will be addressed in Chapter 4 for triplets and Chapter 5 for doublets. Whenever needed for further information, lexicographic data are complemented with corpus data.

3.6.1.2 Past competition

As mentioned above, 68 clusters, i.e., 19 %, are classified as past competition, in which none of the competitors remains in use. For example, in the cluster *oracle/oraclize* ('speak as an oracle'), both competitors are tagged as 'rare' or 'obsolete' in the OED (Tab. 13). Specifically, the converted form is latest attested in the 19th century, while its competitor in *-ize* is latest attested at the beginning of the 18th century. No records for any of the forms are found in the corpora consulted.

Tab. 13. An example of past competition

Lemma	S	Semantic category	Definition	Status	*	†
oracle	2	SIMILATIVE	speak as an oracle	rare	1654	1866
oraclize	2		speak as an oracle	obs	1709	1709

This has been set apart from the clusters showing resolved competition, where at least one of the members remains in use, because the end of competition is a consequence of the decay in the use of both forms. The reasons for the unavailability of all the forms in the cluster may be due to various factors:

i) Low frequency: *oraclize* is recorded only once in the OED, which may indicate that it was never a frequent form.[29] This is also supported by the lack of records in corpora.

29 In fact, the OED only provides a quotation that attest the existence of *oraclize*: *Then shall Thy Conscience Oraclise thy Fate* [1648, Earl of Westmorland *Otia Sacra* (1879) 57].

ii) Change in the historico-cultural context: both *melancholy* and *melancholized* compete for the sense 'make melancholy' (which is no longer in use).
iii) The existence of a form with a different base: all the forms in the cluster *perfection/perfectionate/perfectionize* ('bring to perfection') are tagged as rare in the OED, possibly because at the moment of their attestation the sense was already expressed by a well-attested form (i.e., *perfect* 'bring to perfection') (see Section 4.3.3 for a more detailed analysis).

3.6.1.3 Ongoing competition

Although the results suggest that most cases of competition are expected to be ultimately resolved, the time resolution may take to be complete is variable and competition may remain unresolved at present (Fernández-Alcaina 2017). This is evidenced by the categories ORNATIVE and STATIVE in the cluster *character/characterize*. A total of 110 clusters, i.e., 32 %, have been classified as instances of 'ongoing competition', e.g., *aerosol/aerosolize* (Tab. 14):

Tab. 14. An example of ongoing competition

Lemma	S	Semantic category	Definition	Status	*	†
aerosol	1	RESULTATIVE	= *aerosolize*, v1	in use	1964	1998
aerosolize	1		make into an aerosol	in use	1944	2001

3.6.2 Profile of resolution

The profile displayed by the resolution of competition in the clusters analysed is highly heterogenous as regards both the duration of competition and the form (i.e., earliest or latest attested) that wins such competition. The remaining of the section describes the duration of competition, the form that remains in use and the direction of the resolution of competition.

3.6.2.1 Variable duration of competition

As argued by Aronoff (2019: 47), competition is ultimately expected to be resolved, although the time it may take may be variable. In some clusters, competition is attested to last for centuries (e.g., *beauty/beautify* 'make beauty', Fig. 9)

Examples like this, in which one of the competitors has been recorded only once in the OED are labeled here as cases of 'incidental competition' (see section 3.6.2.1).

while in others it is short-lived and resolved within the same century in which the forms have been are first attested (e.g., *method*/*methodize* 'arrange methodically', Fig. 9).

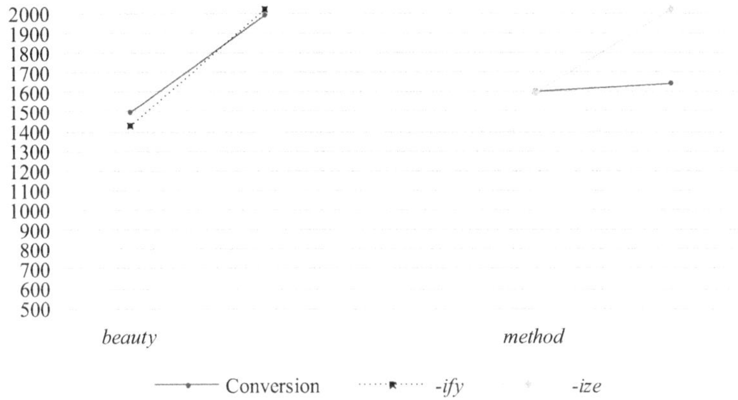

Fig. 9. Example of variable duration of competition

It must be noted that, in some cases, one of the competitors is attested only once in the OED. As Allan (2012: 26, footnote 6) concludes, '[s]ince the earliest and latest available quotations are given for each sense, a single quotation suggests that no others have been found'. In fact, in the doublets where this occurs (labeled here as 'incidental competition'), the later attested form is always marked as 'obsolete' for the sense in competition (e.g., *powder*/*powderize*, *mist*/*misten*, *palsy*/*palsify*, *nullify*/*nullize* or *mylinate*/*mylinize*).

Remarkably, in those doublets where conversion and affixation compete, competition is resolved in favor of conversion (Tab. 15):

Tab. 15. Examples of incidental competition classified as resolved competition[a]

Earliest attested verb		**Incidental competitor**	
action	1734–1996	*actionize*	1871–1871
alkalize	1666–2000	*alkali*	1849–1849
pattern	1567–2001	*patternize*	1615–1615
raven	1570–2006	*ravenize*	1677–1677
station	1609–2009	*stationize*	1598–1598
powder	1616–2002	*powderize*	1800–1800
humour	1598–1982	*humorize*	1598–1598
peacock	1654–1990	*peacockize*	1598–1598
wanton	1634–2011	*wantonize*	1673–1673
petition	1611–1994	*petitionate*	1625–1625
mist	1439–1994	*misten*	1599–1599
root	1450–1998	*rooten*	1652–1652
palsy	1615–2003	*palsify*	1882–1882

a For easier reading, the number of the sense with which they are listed in the OED is not specified here.

There is one exception to the above: the doublet *alkali/alkalize*, in which the prevalence of the *-ize* suffixed verb may be explained by the influence of French. As noted by the OED, *alkalize* is apparently modeled on the French form *alcaliser*, which is already attested in French with this sense in 1628 in its participial form.[30]

In any case, that some forms are recorded only once in the OED raise questions about the classification of such clusters as instances of competition. It is doubtful that they could qualify as competitors since no coexistence can be attested. While a unique quotation in the OED may be a result of the difficulty of accessing written materials, which is subject to the availability of new resources in a future, the attestation of 'incidental competitors' seems to be rather the by-product of the inclusive policy followed by the OED. This includes rare or nonce forms with the same meaning of an already attested form, possible due to reasons of prestige or personal innovation, which did not however have an effect on the existence of a previous existing form. Examples like this show that, given the

30 *Alkalize* competes with *alkalify* for the sense 'make alkaline' and also with other verbs which have a different base (*alkalinize*) or which are described as borrowed elements (*alkalizate*) in the OED.

heterogeneity of the profile displayed by competition, its study requires an individual analysis of the features of each cluster. Such variability is also observed in the direction resolution may take, as described in Section 3.6.2.2.

3.6.2.2 *Direction of resolution*

3.6.2.2.1 *Earliest vs latest attested competitor*

As suggested by the results obtained in the competition in triplets and doublets, clusters displaying resolved competition outnumber those where all the forms are attested to be in use in Present-Day English according to the OED. This section elaborates on the profiles of such resolution according to the prevailing competitor in terms of attestation dates. Specifically:

i) Clusters where the later attested competitor prevails by replacing an already attested verb (e.g., *less/lessen*, *statue/statufy*, *mirrorize/mirror*) (Fig. 10).

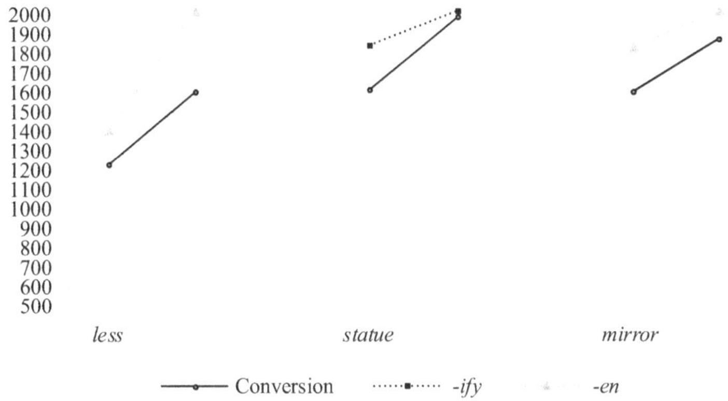

Fig. 10. The latest attested competitor replaces an already existing form

ii) Clusters in which the earliest attested form remains after the appearance of a competitor (e.g., *parrot/parrotize*, *terror/terrify*, *culture/culturate*) (Fig. 11).

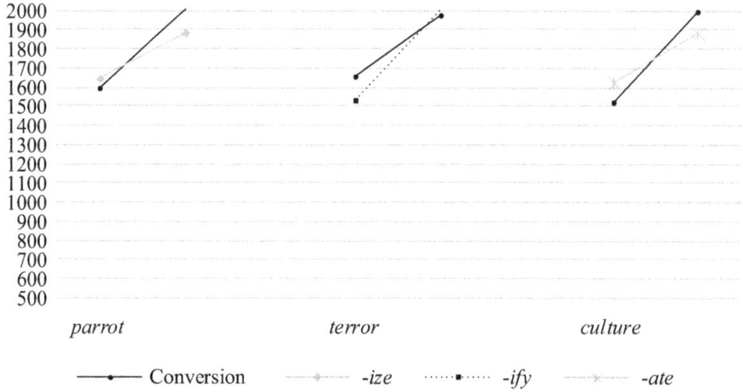

Fig. 11. The earliest attested competitor remains in use despite the appearance of a later form

3.6.2.2.2 Pattern-governed vs lexically-governed

Resolution is, independently of the patterns of competition or the semantic categories expressed, the most common outcome of competition. The shape it may take is in most cases unclear. A priori, the competition between individual words would resolve in favor of the earliest attested form (by blocking), while the competition between word-formation patterns would be expected to be resolved in favor of the latest attested form (Bauer 2006: 181).

Regarding the patterns of the competition under study, the latest attested form prevails over the earliest attested form in the competition between conversion and *-en* suffixation. Fig. 12 shows the timelines for the competition of conversion and *-en* suffixation classified by the pattern that prevails.

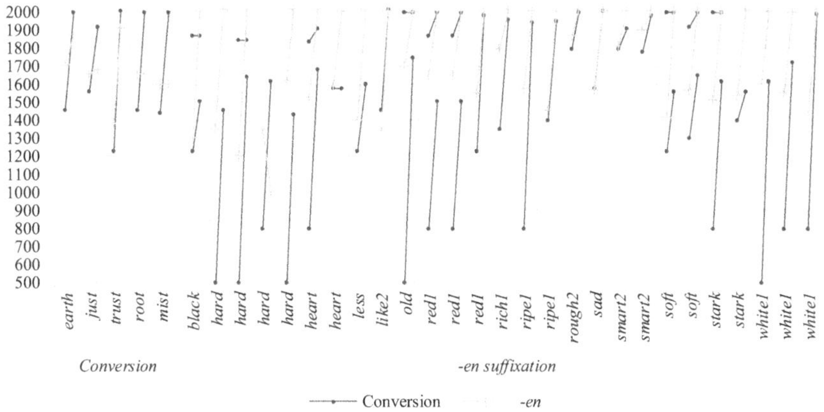

Fig. 12. Timeline for the competition between conversion (dark grey line) and *-en* suffixation (light grey line) classified by prevailing process

The number of clusters in which conversion prevails over *-en* suffixation is restricted to five, all of them classified as denominal formation (i.e., *earth/earthen*, *just/justen*, *trust/trusten*, *root/rooten* and *mist/misten*). In contrast, in the rest of the clusters displaying resolved competition, resolution occurs in favor of *-en* suffixation. In fact, the timelines represented in Fig. 12 show a general replacement of the converted verbs by *-en* suffixed competitors. In some cases, a later converted form is attested, although in most cases it seems to be short-lived (e.g, *heart/hearten*, *red/redden*, *soft/soften*) or even incidental (e.g., *black/blacken*, *old/olden* or *stark/starken*).

In other clusters, however, the resolution of competition does not seem to follow a specific pattern, partly as a consequence of the influence of borrowing and analogy. For example, the competition in clusters expressing classified as ORNATIVE in the sample is usually resolved in favor of the converted form (e.g., *artery/arterize* 'provides with arteries', *companion/companionize* 'provide with a companion' or *powder/powderize* 'apply powder', among others). However, as described above, competition in the cluster *alkali/alkalize* ('impregnate with alkali') is resolved in favor of the *-ize* suffixed verb, possible influenced by the French form *alkaliser*.

3.7 Summary

The heterogeneity displayed by the clusters collected in the sample affects various levels of the description of competition.

Regarding the form, the patterns identified vary widely, even if conversion is present in most of the verbal clusters, followed by *-ize* suffixation. The results obtained in this regard agree with the alleged productivity of the two processes in verbal derivation (Plag 1999).

As regards the meaning, an overview of the semantic categories of the clusters does not seem to provide much conclusive evidence about the competing patterns. Competition is attested in ten semantic categories unevenly distributed among the patterns identified, CAUSATIVE, ORNATIVE and RESULTATIVE being the three categories with the highest number of clusters. However, while the CAUSATIVE category is mainly expressed by clusters where conversion competes with *-en* suffixation, the results obtained for ORNATIVE clusters show, a priori, a more even distribution among the patterns.

The heterogenous nature of competition also extends to its resolution. An individual analysis of the clusters allows for the identification of various profiles of resolution regarding the duration of competition, the preference for an earliest or latest attested competitor and also the direction of resolution, which may either follow an established pattern or which may differ from other similar clusters due to the influence of external factors, such as borrowing.

Furthermore, this chapter has also provided evidence on the importance of assessing competition at the level of senses, which is crucial for two reasons:

i) It allows to gain insights into the various degrees of synonymy displayed by the clusters analysed: from those where competition is attested in only one of the senses of the forms (e.g., *history/historify/historize*) to those where competition extends over other senses as well (e.g., *character/characterize*).
ii) More importantly, competition between various senses may present different stages of resolution. In this respect, competition is resolved in 49 % of the clusters, while those where competition is attested in Present-Day English amounts to 32 %. The remaining 20 % are clusters in which competition once occurred but where both forms are recorded in the OED as 'obsolete'.

Chapter 4: Triplets

4.1 Introduction

This chapter explores the profile of competition in clusters where three (or, rarely, more than three) verbs compete for the expression of the same category. The rest of the chapter is organized as follows: Section 4.2 provides an overview of the patterns in competition and the categories expressed. Section 4.3 describes the profile of the resolution of competition in this type of clusters. A summary of the main findings is provided in Section 4.4.

4.2 Profile of competition

The number of clusters containing three or more forms extracted from the OED amounts to 31 clusters, i.e., 9 %. Specifically, 30 clusters contain three members (i.e., 8 %), while the competition between more than three forms (i.e., 1 %) is attested in only one cluster (*fossil/fossilate/fossilify/fossilize*).

Despite the fact that most clusters contain a converted or *-ize* suffixed form as a competitor, triplets display great variation as regards the patterns involved in competition (Tab. 16):

Tab. 16. Clusters per pattern and examples

Pattern	%	Clusters	Example
Ø/-ate/-ize	39 %	12	*mission/missionate/missionize*
Ø /-ify/-ize/	29 %	9	*immune/immunify/immunize*
-ate/-ify/-ize	10 %	3	*carbonate/carbonify/carbonize*
Ø /-en/-ify	10 %	3	*moist/moisten/moistify*
Ø /en-/-ize	6 %	2	*empatron/patron/patronize*
Ø /-en/-ize	3 %	1	*quiet/quieten/quietize*
Ø /-ate/-ify/-ize	3 %	1	*fossil/fossilate/fossilify/fossilize*

In line with the results described for the profile of competition outlined in Chapter 3, conversion and *-ize* suffixation are the two most common processes found in competition (i.e., in 28 clusters each), followed by *-ate* (15 clusters) and *-ify* suffixation (12 clusters). Other processes such as *-en* suffixation and *en-* prefixation are found in a low number of clusters (four and one clusters, respectively). No examples of clusters with three or more forms in which *be-* prefixation is one of the competitors are identified in the sample.

Regarding the semantics of competition in triplets, the semantic categories identified in the sample are the following:

i) CAUSATIVE (eleven triplets, i.e., 35 %)
ii) RESULTATIVE (nine triplets, i.e., 29 %)
iii) ORNATIVE (three triplets, i.e., 10 %)
iv) PERFORMATIVE (three triplets, i.e., 10 %)
v) SIMILATIVE (two triplets, i.e., 6 %)
vi) INCHOATIVE (one triplet, i.e., 3 %)
vii) LOCATIVE (one triplet, i.e., 3 %)

4.3 Resolution of competition

4.3.1 Introduction

Following the definitions and the attestation dates provided by the OED, the profile of competition displayed by the clusters is the following (Fig. 13):

i) 20 clusters, i.e., 64 %, show resolved competition, either completely (14 triplets, i.e., 45 %) or partially (six triplets, i.e., 19 %);
ii) eight clusters, i.e., 26 %, display ongoing competition as their members are unmarked regarding status in the OED;
iii) three clusters, i.e., 10 %, contain members marked as 'obsolete' or 'rare' in the OED.

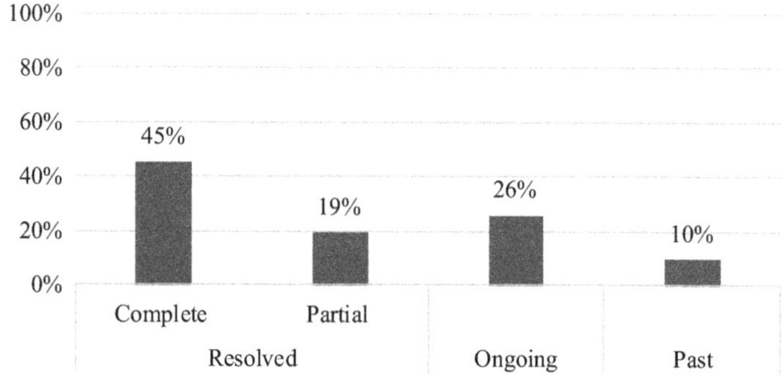

Fig. 13. Profile of competition in clusters with three or more members

Each of the outcomes of the resolution of competition in triplets are described in more detail in Sections 4.3.2–4.3.3.

4.3.2 Resolved competition

This section elaborates on the clusters displaying resolved competition (either completely or partially). The aim is to confirm whether there exist patterns of resolution that are common to various clusters or whether, by contrast, the resolution of competition is unique to each cluster. In particular, this section focuses on the resolution of competition in clusters where *-ize* suffixation is one of the competitors, as it appears in 17 of the 20 triplets where resolution occurs, i.e., 85 %.[31]

The results obtained suggest that both possibilities are not mutually exclusive. Specifically, Section 4.3.2.1 focuses on the clusters where, independently of the semantic category and the affixes in competition, *-ize* suffixation prevails over the rest of its competitors. Section 4.3.2.2 presents a number of clusters where the resolution of competition seems to be a consequence of the influence of other factors, such as borrowing (e.g., *personify*), or semantically related forms (e.g., *passivate*).

4.3.2.1 -ize *suffixation*

-ize suffixation acts as a competitor in 17 of the 20 triplets displaying complete or partial resolution, i.e., 85 %, where it remains in use in eight of the 17 clusters regardless of the semantic category expressed, i.e., 47 % (Tab. 17):

31 In the remaining three clusters, the competing pattern is conversion/*-en*/*-ify* (*moist*/*moisten*/*moistify*, *neat*/*neaten*/*neatify*).

Tab. 17. Triplets (or above) with resolved competition where *-ize* suffixation remains in use

Lemma	S	Semantic category	Status	*	†
carbonate2	2	RESULTATIVE	obsolete	1799	1831
carbonify	2		rare	1801	1984
carbonize	1		in use	1798	-
missionate	-	PERFORMATIVE	now rare	1815	1966
missionize	1		in use	1826	-
mission	2b		obs rare	1898	1898
immune	-	CAUSATIVE	rare	1849	1989
immunize	1a		Medicine and Biology	1889	-
immunify	-		rare (now disused)	1892	1905
pollen	-	ORNATIVE	poetic	1877	1983
pollinate	1		in use	1873	-
pollinize	-		chiefly North American	1873	-
pauper	-	RESULTATIVE	in use	1841	-
pauperize	-		in use	1834	-
pauperate	-		obsolete	1839	1839
empatron	-	SIMILATIVE	rare	1609/ 1904	2010
patron	-		in use	1624	-
patronize	1a		in use	1593	-
heroify	-	SIMILATIVE	in use	1677	-
heroize	1a		in use	1695	-
heroize	1b		in use	1887	-
hero	-		rare	1762	1992
fossil	-	RESULTATIVE	chiefly in *passive*	1750	-
fossilize	2a		present (usually in passive)	1794	-
fossilize	3b		in use	1848	-
fossilate	-		rare	1822	1972
fossilify	-		rare	1843	1969

As shown in Tab. 17, *-ize* suffixation prevails over the rest of competitors, as it is the only verb attested to be in use according to the OED in three of the eight clusters, where the other two competitors are marked as 'obsolete' or 'rare' for this sense (*carbonize, missionize, immunize*).

Competition is resolved by specialization in the cluster *pollen/pollinate/pollinize*. The converted form (*pollen*) is marked as 'poetic', while the verb in *-ize* (*pollinize*) is marked as dialectal ('chiefly North American').

In other clusters, *-ize* suffixation allegedly remains in use alongside another competitor where competition has been partially resolved (*pauper/pauperize*, *patron/patronize*, *heroify/heroize* and *fossil/fossilize*). However, a look at the paradigms formed by the competing forms shows that the *-ize* verb allows further derivation in the four clusters, for example in the case of *pauperize* (Tab. 18). This alleged bias towards *-ize* suffixation is further supported by corpus data (Tab. 19).

Tab. 18. Derivatives as support for the prevalence of *-ize* suffixation over conversion in the cluster *pauper/pauperate/pauperize*[a]

pauper	*pauper*	1841	2002				
	pauperize	1806	-	*pauperized*	Adj	1807	-
				pauperizer	N	1826	2016
				pauperizing	Adj	1817	-
				pauperization	N	1812	-
	pauperate	1839	1839				

a Competition in the cluster *pauper/pauperize* is discussed in previous research (Fernández-Alcaina 2017; Fernández-Alcaina & Čermák 2018).

Tab. 19. Corpus data for clusters showing partial resolution

	EHCB		COHA		COCA		iWeb
fossil	-	-	-	-	-	-	-
fossilize	-	-	51	0.13	190	0.19	1637
fossilate	-	-	-	-	-	-	-
fossilify	-	-	-	-	-	-	-
pauper	-	-	-	-	-	-	-
pauperize	-	-	32	0.08	6	0.01	-
pauperate	-	-	-	-	-	-	-
empatron	-	-	-	-	-	-	-
patron	-	-	-	-	-	-	-
patronize	1700	1.72	1355	3.35	1389	1.4	7078
hero	-	-	-	-	-	-	-
heroify	1	>0.01	-	-	-	-	-
heroize	-	-	-	1	0.0	-	-

4.3.2.2 Special cases

In the remaining nine clusters where *-ize* suffixation appears as one of the competitors, several factors could explain the various outcomes observed in the resolution of competition. Some of the clusters are described below for illustration of the influence of several variables on morphological competition.

4.3.2.2.1 External influence: *function* and *personify*

The same competing pattern is observed in the three triplets *function/functionate/functionize*, *mission/missionate/missionize* and *pauper/pauperate/pauperize*, except that with an opposite resolution. Despite similarities regarding their bases (nominal Latinate trochaic bases), competition in the cluster *function/functionate/functionize* is resolved in favor of conversion, which can be partly explained by the influence of French. As the OED notes, the French verb *fonctionner* (1787; 1637 as *functionner*) is attested earlier (Tabs. 20 and 21).

Tab. 20. Lexicographic data for the triplet *function/functionate/functionize*

Lemma	S	Semantic category	Definition	Status	*	†
function	1a		fulfil one's function	in use	1844	-
functionate	-	PERFORMATIVE	fulfil one's function	now rare	1843	1961
functionize	-		fulfil one's function	obs, rare	1847	1927

Tab. 21. Corpus data for the triplet *function/functionate/functionize*

	EBCH		COHA		COCA		iWeb
function	163	0.17	4002	9.88	20370	20.51	360237
functionate	-	-	-	-	-	-	-
functionize	-	-	-	-	-	-	-

French influence may also be a possible reason for the resolution of competition in favor of *-ify* suffixation in the triplets *personate/personify/personize*. In this case, the OED notes that *personify* is 'modelled on a French lexical item'. This is also reflected in the derivatives based on this sense (Tabs. 22 and 23).

Tab. 22. Lexicographic information for the triplet *personify/personate/personize*

Lemma	S	Semantic category	Definition	Status	*	†
personify	1		represent or imagine as a person	in use	1728	-
personate	6	RESULTATIVE	represent or imagine as a person	rare	1612/ 1823	1997
personize	2		represent as a person; *personify*	rare	1726	1846

Tab. 23. Derivatives supporting the prevalence of *-ify* suffixation over *-ate* and *ize* suffixa tion in the triplet *personate/personify/personize*

*personify*1	1728	1989	represent as a person	*personifiable*	1890	1996			
				*personified*1	1753	2001	*unpersonified*	1775	2013
				personification	1728	2003	*personaficative*	1890	1983
							personificator	1834	1989
				*personifier*1	1805	1984			
				personifying	1728	1992			
				personifying	1804	1991			
				dispersonify	1846	1855			
*personize*2	1726	1846	= *personify*						
*personate*6	1612	1997	= *personify*	*personation*3	1832	1989			

4.3.2.2.2 *Internal influence: passivate/passivify/passivize*

For the CAUSATIVE triplet *passivate/passivify/passivize* ('make metal unreactive'), lexicographic data point at the resolution of competition in favor of *-ate* suffixation (Tab. 24):

Tab. 24. Lexicographic information for the triplet *passivate/passivify/passivize*

Lemma	S	Semantic category	Definition	Status	*	†
passivate	1		make (metal) unreactive	Metallurgy and Chemistry	1913	-
passivify	-	CAUSATIVE	= *passivate*, v.1	Manufacturing, rare	1907	1934
passivize	1		= *passivate*, v.1	Manufacturing, rare	1910	1983

Resolution in favor of the *-ate* form in this cluster may be explained by the influence of a semantically related form. As the OED notes, both *passivate* ('make unreactive') and *passivation* ('process or action of passivating a metal') have been formed after *activate* ('make more reactive') and *activation* ('process of making a substance more chemically or catalytically active'), respectively. As a result, the initial resolution observed between *-ate* suffixation, *-ify* suffixation and *-ize* suffixation is in favor of the former, resulting in the obsolescence of *passivify*. The *-ize* verb, on the other hand, is restricted to the domain of *Grammar* meaning 'be converted/convert to the passive voice'. Notably, competition extends to the forms in their derivational paradigm (Tab. 25).

Tab. 25. Derivation paradigm for the triplet *passivate/passivify/passivize*

*passivate*1	1913	1992	Metallurgy	*passivated*	1919	1992	Manufacturing Technology
				passivating	1914	1986	Manufacturing Technology
				passivating	1918	1993	Manufacturing Technology
				passivation	1912	1999	Manufacturing Technology
				passivator	1935	1996	Manufacturing Technology
*passivate*2	1964	1998	Electronics				
*passivize*1	1910	1983	Manufacturing Technology, rare	*passivizing*1	1975	1075	Metallurgy, rare
*passivize*2	1965	1984	Grammar				
*passivize*2b	1972	2002	Grammar	*passivizable*	1972	1990	Grammar
				passivizability	1967	1999	Grammar
				passivization	1965	1991	Grammar
				passivized	1975	2001	Grammar
				*passivizing*2	1977	2002	Various
passivify	1907	1934	Manufacturing Technology, rare	*passivification*	1907	1937	Manufacturing Technology, rare
				passivified	1911	1934	Manufacturing Technology, rare
				passivifier	1911	1921	Manufacturing Technology, rare
				passivifying	1907	1907	Manufacturing Technology, rare
				passivifying	1915	1938	Manufacturing Technology, rare

4.3.3 Past competition

Another reason for the resolution of competition among the members of the same cluster may be the existence of a lexical competitor, which may be morphologically related or not. Thus, the verbs in the triplet *perfection/perfectionate/perfectionize* ('bring to perfection') compete with the earlier attested verb *perfect*. The three morphological competitors are marked as 'rare' in the OED (Tab. 26).

Tab. 26. Lexicographic information for the triplet *perfection/perfectionate/perfectionize*

Lemma	S	Semantic category	Definition	Status	*	†
perfect	2		make perfect; bring to perfection	in use	1440	-
perfection	-	CAUSATIVE	bring to perfection	rare	1651	1999
perfectionate	-		bring to perfection	now rare	1570	1993
perfectionize	-		bring to perfection	now rare	1805	1997

This is also supported by the information available in synchronic dictionaries (*Collins* and *Merriam-Webster*) for the verbs recorded (*perfectionate* and *perfectionize*) (Tab. 27):

Tab. 27. Lexicographic information for the triplet *perfection/perfectionate/perfectionize*

	Collins	*Merriam-Webster*
perfection	-	-
perfectionate	(rare) perfect; make perfect	(archaic) = *perfect*
perfectionize	-	(archaic) = perfect

4.3.4 Ongoing competition

Corpus data and derivational paradigms have proved to provide further information on the competition of triplets. Not only where lexicographic information points at a resolution towards a specific form (e.g., *carbonate/carbonize/carbonify*) but also in the clusters that display partial competition (e.g., *pauper/pauperate/pauperize, fossil/fossilate/fossilify/fossilize*), i.e., where two of the competitors were attested as in use by the OED. Both corpora and the study of their derivatives have provided further data on a tentative preference for one of the forms.

However, since the resolution of competition takes time, there are also clusters for which there is no way to identify a bias towards any of the forms involved. In some cases, such unresolved competition extends to the derivatives. Consider the example *patine/patinate/patinize*, where the verbs compete for the sense 'cover with a patina' and where both competitors and derivatives are attested as in use in the OED (Tab. 28):

Tab. 28. Derivational paradigm for the triplet *patine/patinate/patinize*

patine	1896	-	= *patinate*	*patining*	1939	-	= *patinating*
patinate	1867	-	cover with a patina	*patinated*	1893	-	covered with a patina
				patinating	1914	-	process of covering with a patina
patination	1888	-	the condition of having a patina				
patinize	1948	-	= *patinate*	*patinizing*	1904	-	= *patinating*

The corpora used do not provide much information regarding the competition, possibly as a consequence of the use of the forms in a specialized domain (Tab. 29):

Tab. 29. Corpus data for the triplet *patine/patinate/patinize*

	EHCB		COHA		COCA		iWeb
patine	-	-	-	-	-	-	-
patinate	-	-	2	0	8	0.01	-
patinize	na	-	-	-	-	-	-

4.4 Summary

The existence of clusters with three or more forms is relatively low, compared with the number of doublets identified. Although most of the clusters identified show a preference for suffixation *-ize* to prevail, other clusters illustrate how a series of factors, e.g., borrowing (e.g., *personify*), related forms (e.g., *activate/passivate*) or the existence of another form with the same sense (e.g., *perfect*) may interfere in morphological competition. Despite the number of triplets is low, these results here provide further evidence on the heterogeneity of the competition described in Chapter 3 and on the need of an individual analysis of clusters.

Methodologically, both corpus data and derivational paradigms have proved to serve as further evidence for the study of competition in some clusters, such as *fossil/fossilize* or *pauper/pauperize*. Similarly, synchronic dictionaries may also help to shed light on the use of competitors, to support either resolved competition (e.g., *perfection/perfectionate/perfectionize*) or unresolved competition (e.g., *patine/patinate/patinize*).

Chapter 5: Doublets

5.1 Introduction

This chapter elaborates on the competition of verbal doublets. Of the 319 doublets identified in the sample:

i) 273 doublets, i.e., 85 %, have conversion as one of the competitors, and
ii) 46 doublets, i.e., 15 %, show competition between suffixed forms.

Since conversion is present in most of the doublets identified, the description of competition in the remaning of the chapter is divided into two parts. Specifically, Section 5.2 focuses on the competition between conversion and affixation. Section 5.3 elaborates on the clusters where both competitors are derived by suffixation. The main findings for the competition in doublets are summarized in Section 5.4.

5.2 Conversion vs affixation

Most of the doublets extracted in this sample belong to instances of conversion vs affixation. Independently of semantic category, the most common competitor of conversion is *-ize* suffixation, which is only to be expected considering they are the two most common verb-forming processes in English (Plag 1999). Specifically:

i) Doublets where conversion competes with *-ize* suffixation amount to 129 clusters, i.e., 47 %.
ii) Competition vs *-en* suffixation amounts to 70 doublets, i.e., 26 %.
iii) The two remaining suffixes identified in the sample amount to 48 doublets, i.e., 20 %. In particular:
    a) Competition with *-ate* suffixation amounts to 22 doublets, i.e., 8 %.
    b) Competition with *-ify* suffixation amounts to 26 clusters, i.e., 10 %.
iv) The number of doublets where conversion competes with prefixation is marginal:
    a) 19 doublets, i.e., 7 %, have an *en*-prefixed verb as a competitor for conversion.
    b) Seven doublets, i.e., 3 %, have a *be*-prefixed verb as a competitor for conversion.

In terms of semantic classification, competition is highly heterogeneous regarding the semantic category for which the verbs compete. Semantic distribution is illustrated in Fig. 14:

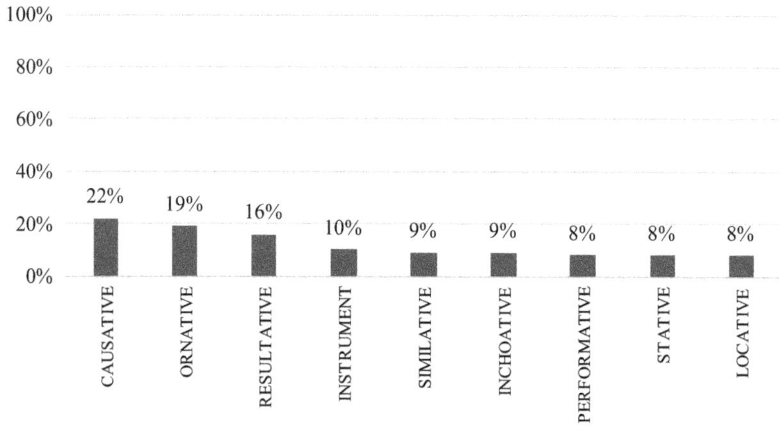

Fig. 14. Semantic categories expressed by doublets where conversion is in competition with affixation. The category PRIVATIVE is not represented as it is only represented by one cluster (>1 %).

None of the categories in which competition occurs clearly stands out from the rest, as doublets are evenly distributed across semantic categories, as the values for the three most common semantic categories illustrate:

i) CAUSATIVE (61 clusters, i.e., 22 %)
ii) ORNATIVE (53 clusters, i.e., 19 %)
iii) RESULTATIVE (44 clusters, i.e., 16 %)

As expected, the category with the lowest number of competing clusters is one of the least common also in previous research (e.g., Gottfurcht 2008; Valera 2020) (PRIVATIVE).

However, the fact that clusters are evenly distributed across semantic categories does not imply that they are equally represented by all affixes. A look at the five most common semantic categories in the doublets analysed (Fig. 14) shows that, while CAUSATIVE and INCHOATIVE are the two most typical categories in clusters where conversion competes with *-en* suffixation, the categories INSTRUMENT, ORNATIVE, PERFORMATIVE and SIMILATIVE are the most common categories expressed by the clusters of conversion vs *-ize* suffixation.

Competition for the expression of the semantic categories represented seems to be restricted to a particular pattern:

i) Conversion vs *-en* suffixation in the categories CAUSATIVE and INCHOATIVE.
ii) Conversion vs *-ize* suffixation in the categories INSTRUMENT, ORNATIVE, PERFORMATIVE, RESULTATIVE, SIMILATIVE and STATIVE.
iii) Unlike the rest of categories governed by the competition between conversion and *-ize* suffixation, ORNATIVE doublets obtain more even values irrespective of the patters in competition.

5.2.1 Conversion vs *-ize* suffixation

A total of 129 clusters show competition between conversion and *-ize* suffixation:

i) 26 doublets, i.e., 20 %, express the category RESULTATIVE (e.g., *powder/powderize* 'reduce to powder').
ii) 22 doublets, i.e., 17 %, express the category SIMILATIVE (e.g., *parrot/parrotize* 'repeat words mindlessly').
iii) 20 doublets, i.e., 15 %, express the category ORNATIVE (e.g., *artery/arterize* 'provide with arteries').
iv) 18 doublets, i.e., 14 %, express the category INSTRUMENT (e.g., *adjective/adjectivize* 'qualify using adjectives').
v) 18 doublets, i.e., 14 %, express the category PERFORMATIVE (e.g., *monologue/monologuize* 'talk in monologue').
vi) 15 doublets, i.e., 12 %, express the category CAUSATIVE (e.g., *savage/savagize* 'make savage').
vii) Six doublets, i.e., 5 % express the category SIMILATIVE (e.g., *parrot/parrotize* 'repeat words mechanically (as a parrot)')
viii) Three doublets, i.e., 2 %, express the category INCHOATIVE (e.g., *powder/powderize* 'become powder')

Regarding the resolution of competition between conversion and *-ize* suffixation:

i) 52 doublets, i.e., 40 %, are classified as resolved competition by:
   a) Obsolescence of one of the forms with the competing sense (e.g., *hazard/hazardize* 'put in danger or jeopardy') (47 doublets, i.e., 90 %), and
   b) Specialization (e.g., *verbal/verbalize* 'talk, speak', where the converted form is marked as *colloquial* by the OED) (five doublets, i.e., 10 %).
ii) 50 doublets, i.e., 39 %, show ongoing competition, as both forms are attested in Present-Day English (e.g., *adjective/adjectivize* 'qualify using adjectives').

iii) 27 doublets, i.e., 21 %, are instances of past competition (e.g., *epicure/epicurize* 'indulge oneself by luxurious living').

For those clusters classified as diplaying resolved competition, Fig. 15 shows the prevalence of each process by semantic category:

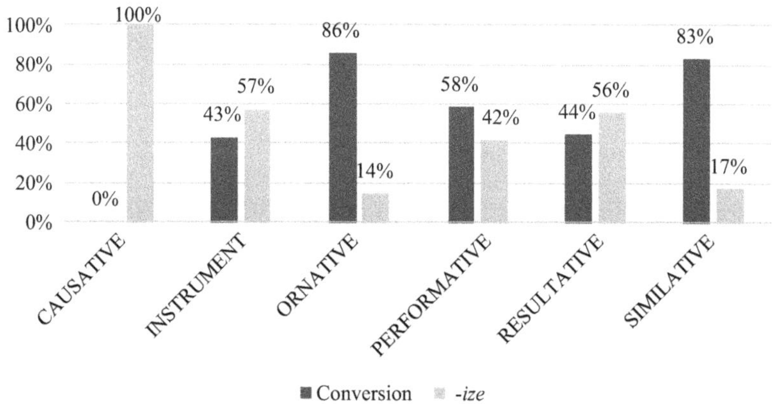

Fig. 15. Resolved competition in favor of conversion (dark grey) or *-ize* suffixation (light grey). Only categories with more than five clusters have been included

Of the eight semantic categories identified in doublets with resolved competition:

i) *-ize* suffixation prevails over conversion for the expression of:
   a) CAUSATIVE (nine doublets, i.e., 100 %) (e.g., *parallel/parallelize* 'make parallel'),
   b) INSTRUMENT (four doublets, i.e., 57 %) (e.g., *signal/signalize* 'communicate by means of signals'), and
   c) RESULTATIVE (five doublets, i.e., 59 %) (e.g., *atom/atomize* 'reduce to atoms').

ii) In ORNATIVE doublets, conversion prevails over suffixation in six doublets, i.e., 86 % (e.g., *alkali/alkalize* 'treat with alkali').

iii) Conversion prevails in five doublets, i.e., 83 % of SIMILATIVE (e.g., *satellite/satellize* 'accompany someone as or like a satellite').

iv) Conversion prevails in seven doublets, i.e., 58 % for the category PERFORMATIVE (e.g., *psalmody/psalmodize* 'sing psalms').

Therefore, the semantic classification of competitors in doublets involving competition between conversion and *-ize* suffixation allows a better understanding of the cases in which one or the other competitor prevails. However, the low number of clusters for each category hinders any attempt of generalization. The following section examines whether a preference for one or the other pattern may be observed in those clusters where competition is unresolved, based on lexicographic data.

5.2.2 Conversion vs *-en* suffixation

Conversion vs *-en* suffixation is the second most frequent pattern identified in the sample. Specifically, this type of competition amounts to 70 doublets distributed into seven semantic categories (Fig. 16):

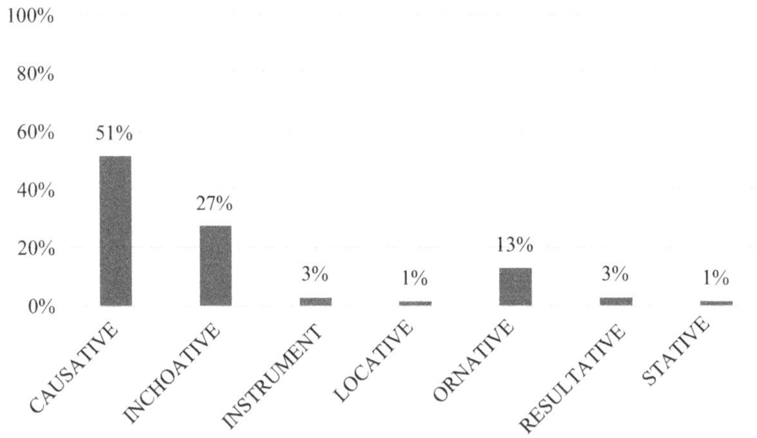

Fig. 16. The semantic distribution of doublets of competition between conversion and *-en* suffixation

The semantic classification of the doublets shows that:

i) 36 doublets, i.e., 51 %, express the category CAUSATIVE.
ii) 19 doublets, i.e., 27 %, express the category INCHOATIVE.
iii) Nine doublets, i.e., 13 %, express the category ORNATIVE.
iv) Competition for the rest of the categories represented (i.e., INSTRUMENT, LOCATIVE, RESULTATIVE and STATIVE) is considered to be marginal.

Fig. 17 shows the profile of competition in doublets of competition between conversion and *-en* suffixation:

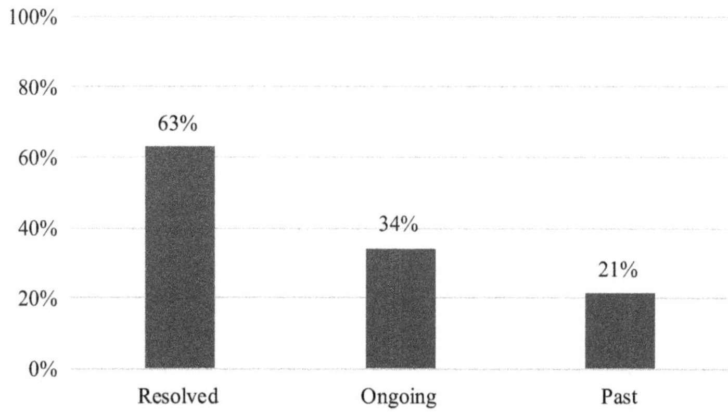

Fig. 17. The profile of competition for clusters involving competition between conversion and *-en* suffixation

Of the 70 doublets analysed:

i) 38 doublets, i.e., 63 %, show resolved competition.
ii) 18 doublets, i.e., 34 %, show ongoing competition.
iii) 14 doublets, i.e., 21 %, show past competition.

Regarding the direction in the resolution of competition, *-en* suffixation prevails over conversion in the two most common semantic categories identified (CAUSATIVE, e.g., *red/redden* 'make red', and INCHOATIVE, e.g., *red/redden* 'become red'), as illustrated in Fig. 18:

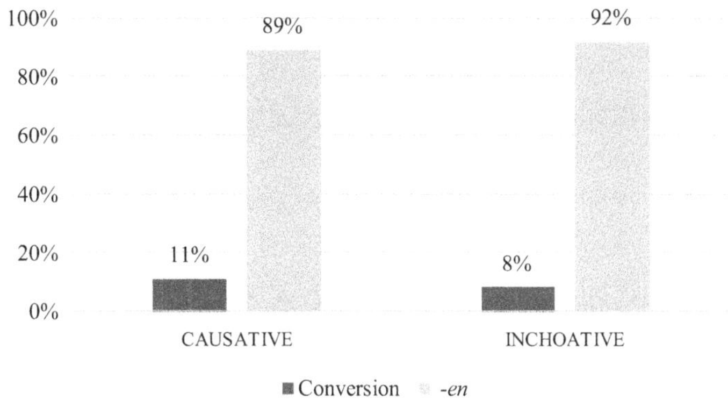

Fig. 18. Resolution in favor of conversion (dark grey) or *-en* suffixation (light grey) for the categories CAUSATIVE and INCHOATIVE

Results show a clear bias towards *-en* suffixation when in competition with conversion. A closer look at the doublets where conversion prevails reveals that:

i) The converted form is attested in Present-Day English, but apparently restricted to a specific variety (e.g., *just* 'adjust for accuracy' is marked as characteristic of Orkney and Shetland). Dialectal differentiation is also observed in other doublets where conversion competes with *-en* suffixation, e.g., *less/lessen*, *piece/piecen*, *sad/sadden*, *smart/smarten*, *stark/starken*, *quiet/quieten*, or *trust/trusten.*
ii) The suffixed verb is a monosemous form, sometimes with only one quotation attested in the OED (e.g., *mist/misten*).

5.2.3 Other cases of competition

5.2.3.1 Conversion vs -ate *suffixation*

Doublets where conversion competes with *-ate* suffixation amount to 21, for which the following five semantic categories are identified:

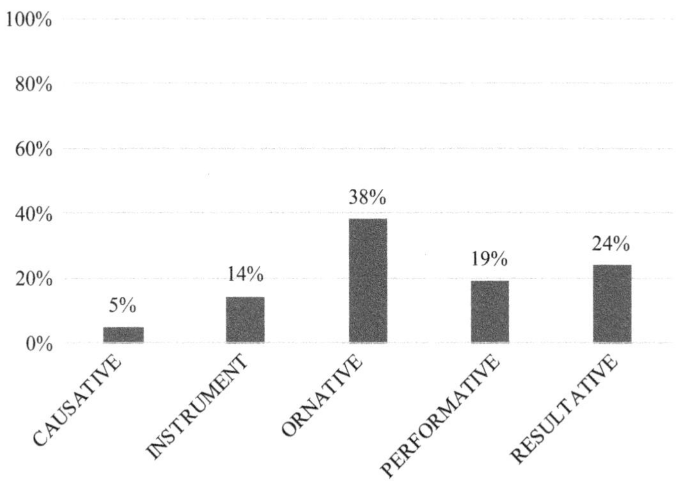

Fig. 19. The semantic distribution of doublets of competition between conversion and *-ate* suffixation

Fig. 19 shows that:

i) Eight doublets, i.e., 38 %, express the category ORNATIVE (e.g., *motive/motivate* 'provide with a motive').
ii) Five doublets, i.e., 24 %, express the category RESULTATIVE (e.g., *faction/factionate* 'make into factions').
iii) Four doublets, i.e., 19 %, express the category PERFORMATIVE (e.g., *culture/culturate* 'cultivate soil, plants').
iv) Three doublets, i.e., 14 %, express the category INSTRUMENT (e.g., *alembic/alembicate* 'distil in an alembic').
v) One doublet, i.e., 5 %, expresses the category CAUSATIVE (e.g., *active/activate* 'distil in an alembic').

Regarding the profile of competition in doublets of competition between conversion and *-ate* suffixation:

i) Eight doublets, i.e., 38 %, show resolved competition for this pattern, with well-balanced results. Specifically, conversion prevails in six, i.e., 75 %, of the eight doublets (e.g., *culture/culturate* 'cultivate (soil, plaints)'), while *-ate* verbs prevail in two, i.e., 25 %, of the eight doublets (e.g., *alembic/alembicate* 'distil in alembic').

ii) Six doublets, i.e., 29 %, show ongoing competition, according to lexicographic data (e.g., *active/activate* 'make active').
iii) Seven doublets, i.e., 33 %, show past competition (e.g., *quintessence/quintessentiate* 'extract the quintessence of or from something').

5.2.3.2 *Conversion vs* -ify *suffixation*

Competition between conversion and *-ify* is attested in 26 doublets, for which the following six semantic categories are identified:

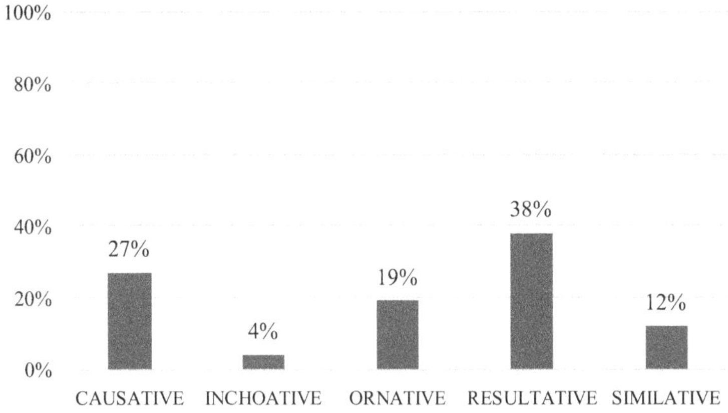

Fig. 20. The semantic distribution of doublets of competition between conversion and *-ify* suffixation

Fig. 20 shows that:

i) Ten doublets, i.e., 38 %, express the category RESULTATIVE.
ii) Seven doublets, i.e., 27 %, express the category CAUSATIVE.
iii) Five doublets, i.e., 19 %, express the category ORNATIVE.
iv) Three doublets, i.e., 12 %, express the category SIMILATIVE.
v) One doublet, i.e., 4 %, expresses the category INCHOATIVE.

As regards the profile of competition in doublets of competition between *-ify* suffixation and *-ize* suffixation:

i) Eleven doublets, i.e., 42 %, show resolved competition (e.g., *beautify/beauty* 'make beautiful'). Specifically:

   a) *-ify* suffixation prevails in six of the eleven doublets, independently of the semantic category.
   b) Conversion prevails in five of the eleven doublets.
- ii) Nine doublets, i.e., 35 %, show ongoing competition (e.g., *dunce/duncify* 'make a dunce of').
- iii) Six clusters, i.e., 23 %, show past competition (e.g., *prince/princify* 'make into a prince').

5.2.3.3 Conversion vs prefixation

Conversion vs *en-* prefixation amounts to 19 doublets, semantically classified as:

- i) Nine doublets, i.e., 47 %, express the category ORNATIVE.
- ii) Three doublets, i.e., 16 %, express the category INSTRUMENT.
- iii) Two doublets, i.e., 11 %, express the category LOCATIVE.
- iv) Two doublets, i.e., 11 %, express the category RESULTATIVE.
- v) One doublet, i.e., 5 %, expresses the category CAUSATIVE.
- vi) One doublet, i.e., 5 %, expresses the category INCHOATIVE.
- vii) One doublet, i.e., 5 %, expresses the category STATIVE.

Regarding the profile of competition between conversion and *-en* suffixation:

- i) Twelve doublets, i.e., 63 %, show resolved competition (e.g., *empower/power* 'make powerful').
- ii) Six doublets, i.e., 32 %, show ongoing competition (e.g., *enqueue/queue* 'place or add in a queue').
- iii) One doublet, i.e., 5 %, shows past competition (e.g., *empride/pride* 'make proud').

Conversion vs *be-* prefixation amounts to only seven doublets (e.g., *belittle/little* 'reduce in size, amount or importance'), classified as STATIVE (two clusters), ORNATIVE (two clusters), CAUSATIVE, PRIVATIVE and SIMILATIVE (one cluster each). Of the seven clusters identified, four of them are classified as past competition (e.g., *belord/lord, bedung/dung*). In those where competition is resolved, in conversion remains in use in two of them: *belord/lord* ('act of behave tyrannically') and *belimb/limb* ('dismember'), while *be-* prefixation prevails for the sense 'reduce in size' in *belittle/little*. However, the low number of clusters identified hinders any attempt of generalization.

5.2.4 Resolution of competition

5.2.4.1 Resolved competition

Fig. 21 shows the resolution of competition between conversion and affixation in doublets. Specifically, competition is resolved in 46 % of the doublets (i.e., 126), where only one of the forms is attested in Present-Day English. Doublets for which there is no resolution of competition amounts to 32 % of the sample (i.e., 88 doublets). Cases of past competition amounts to 22 % of the doublets (i.e., 59 doublets).

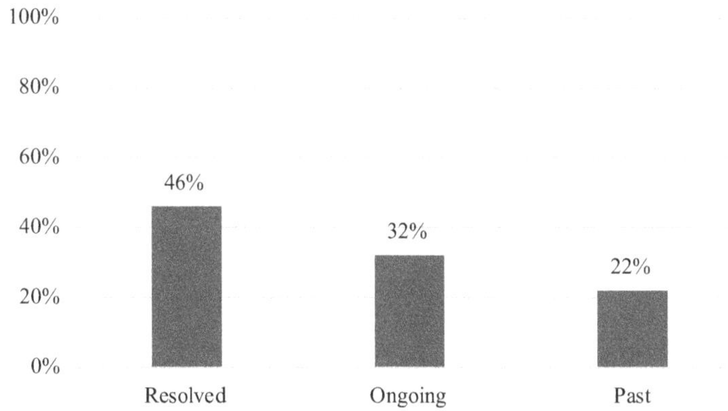

Fig. 21. The profile of competition in doublets where conversion is in competition with affixation

Regarding the direction in which competition is resolved, the results obtained for the competition between conversion and affixation reveals that this may be dependent on the meaning for which they compete. Fig. 22 represents the prevalence of one or the other process in doublets according to their semantic category.

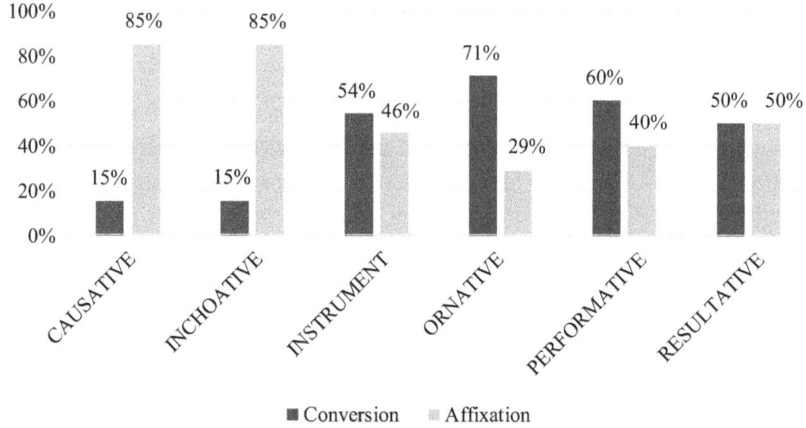

Fig. 22. The resolution of competition in favor of conversion and affixation

Affixation is preferred in only two of the six categories represented. Specifically, resolution in favor of affixation clearly outnumbers conversion for the expression of CAUSATIVE (85 %) and its intransitive counterpart INCHOATIVE (85 %). Opposite resolution may occur within the same clusters. For instance, *wantonize* prevails over *wanton* for the expression of the CAUSATIVE sense, while conversion prevails over *-ize* suffixation for the SIMILATIVE sense. Notably, resolution in the rest of the SIMILATIVE doublets of the competition between conversion and *-ize* suffixation is also in favor of conversion (e.g., *parrot/parrotize, pander/panderize, peacock/peacockize, satellite/satellize*).

In the doublets identified as expressing the categories INSTRUMENT (e.g., *emplaster/plaster*), ORNATIVE (e.g., *companion/companionize*) and PERFORMATIVE (e.g., *photograph/photographize*), in contrast, conversion appears as the prevailing pattern.

For other categories, such as RESULTATIVE (e.g., *hazard/hazardize, signal/signalize, mongrel/mongrelize* or *atom/atomize*), no clear prevalence of one or the other process is observed. This is a consequence of the high degree of polysemy displayed by the clusters in which conversion competes with *-ize* suffixation, as opposed to the rest of patterns of competition.

5.2.4.2 *Past competition*

As already described for the competition in triplets, all the forms in a cluster may be tagged as 'rare' or 'obsolete' because a form with a different base already expresses the same meaning. In other cases, the classification of a cluster as displaying past competition may be simply due to the fact that there is apparently no longer a need for the meaning expressed by the competitors, as in the example *margin/marginate* 'provide with marginal notes' (Tab. 30).

Tab. 30. Past competition in the doublet *margin/marginate*

Lemma	S	Semantic category	Definition	Status	*	†
margin	1	ORNATIVE	provide with marginal notes	obs	1595	1885
marginate	1		provide with marginal notes	obs	1609	1609

5.2.4.3 *Ongoing competition*

The aim of this section is to provide further evidence by combining lexicographic information with corpora and the information provided by the derivational paradigms in which the competitors are allocated. As discussed in Fernández-Alcaina & Čermák (2018) and in Chapter 4 for triplets, lexicographic information may not provide enough evidence for the assessment of certain cases of competition. A look into the derivational paradigms of the forms in competition may provide further information on the resolution of competition. In the doublets where both forms are attested to be in competition at present, derivational paradigms, together with corpus data, synchronic dictionaries and, according to some authors, Google searches, can also shed light on a possible preference for one of the forms in some of the doublets. The cases explained below illustrate this point, thus underlining both the need for combining resources in the study of competition, as well as how this type of studies may be hindered by the lack of available evidence. Insufficient available evidence may be due to:

i) the forms in competition are attested earlier in the 16th or 17th centuries, but the lack of corpus records may indicate their low frequency (e.g., *dunce* (1649)/*duncify* (1594) 'make a dunce of'), or
ii) the forms are attested in the 20th century, so competition may still need time to be resolved (e.g., *acronym* (1967)/*acronymize* (1955) 'convert into an acronym').

The apparently restricted use of some forms to specialized domains (e.g., Mathematics, Manufacturing, Computing, etc.) may also make the study of competition difficult. Thus, the verbs *pellet/pelletize* are defined in the OED as 'form or shape into pellets'. For the nouns denoting the actions of these verbs (*pelleting* and *pelletizing*, formed as *pellet*^{N} + *-ing*), the information provided by the OED may not be enough to establish a difference in use.[32]

The remaining of the section is not intended to provide a detailed classification of the doublets displaying ongoing competition. Rather, the aim is to illustrate the directions competition may take.

5.2.4.3.1 Conversion prevails: pillory/pillorize

An example of a cluster where both competitors are attested as in use in the OED is the doublet *pillory/pillorize*. The verb *pillorize* is recorded in the dictionary as a synonym for *pillory* and latest attested in 2002. The combination of derivational paradigms, corpus data and synchronic dictionaries reveals that:

i) All the derivatives from *pillorize* are marked as 'obsolete' by the OED, except for *pillorization*. However, the OED provides only two quotations for this form, one from 1688 and one from 1998 (Tab. 31).

32 According to the website of FEECO International, a company specialized in providing material for recovery systems, although commonly used interchangeably, *pelleting* and *pelletizing* in fact refer to two well distinguished processes:
Pelleting: 'extrusion process, where cylindrical pellets are formed by forcing material through a die […] Pelleting produces an overall dusty product because the jagged, cylindrical edges rub against each other and break off'.
Pelletizing: 'non-pressure agglomeration method, whereby material fines tumble against each other in the presence of a binding agent. The material fines become tacky, stick together, and pick up more fines as they tumble, in a process known as coalescence'. https://feeco.com/question-week-difference-pelleting-pelletizing/

Tab. 31. Paradigm for *pillory/pillorize*

*pillory*1A	1600	1994	put a person in a pillory	*pilloried*	1671	-	placed in a pillory
				pillorying	1653	-	action/act of punishing a person in a pillory
*pillory*1B	1816	1863	constrict (a person) in a pillory				
pillory2	1699	-	ridicule a person or thing	*pilloried*	1671	-	subjected to public ridicule
				pillorying	1653	-	action/act of exposing a person to public abuse
pillorize	1647	-	= *pillory*, v	*pillorization*	1688/ 1998	1668/ 1998	punishment in a pillory
				pillorized	1656	1656	punished in a pillory
				pillorizing	1720	1891	= *pillorying*
				pillorizing	1890	1890	abusive, defamatory

ii) Corpus data show that conversion prevails (Tab. 32):

Tab. 32. Corpus data for *pillory/pillorize*

	EHCB		COHA		COCA	
pillory	64	0.06	140	0.35	376	0.38
pillorize	3	>0.01	-	-	-	-

iii) *Pillorize* is defined as a synonym for *pillory* in both *Collins* and *Merriam-Webster*, except that it is marked as *archaic* in the former (Tab. 33).

Tab. 33. Lexicographic information for *pillory/pillorize*

	Collins	*Merriam-Webster*
pillory	expose to public ridicule punish by putting in a pillory	set in a pillory as punishment expose to public ridicule
pillorize	archaic: to pillory	: pillory

5.2.4.3.2 Affixation prevails: revolution/revolutionize

The forms in the doublet *revolutionize/revolution* are both recorded as in use in the dictionary. However, only derivatives of the *-ize* verb are attested in the dictionary (Tab. 34).

Tab. 34. Paradigm for *revolution/revolutionize*

revolution	1805	-	*revolutionize*				
*revolutionize*1A	1795	-	make revolutionary	*re-revolutionize*	1803	-	revolutionize again
				revolutionized	1798	-	-
				revolutionizing	1797	-	-
				revolutionizing	1797	-	-
				revolutionizement	1820	1820	-
				revolutionizer	1798	-	-
*revolutionize*1B	1796	-	bring a country under revolutionary form of government				
*revolutionize*1C	1817	1874	engage in revolutionary activity				
*revolutionize*2	1798	-	change a thing completely	*revolutionization*	1871	-	-

This is also supported by the corpus data in Tab. 35, which show that the *-ize* verb is the most frequent form.

Tab. 35. Corpus data for *revolution* and *revolutionize*

	EHCB		COHA		COCA	
revolution	-	-	-	-	-	-
revolutionize	44	0.04	968	2.39	2654	2.67

The fact that there seems to be a bias towards one of the forms does not preclude, however, the possibility that the direction of resolution is reversed in the future or that the form gets to find a niche of lexical specialization. This may be the case of the example described in the next section.

5.2.4.3.3 Semantic specialization: pressure/pressurize

Both these verbs are earliest attested in the 20th century and overlap in the two senses listed in the OED. Specifically, *pressure* is earliest attested in the OED in 1911 with the sense 'apply pressure to, esp. to coerce by applying psychological or moral pressure' in the translation of a speech in the House of Commons of Canada (9):

(9) *Extreme protection brought the formation of gigantic trusts, which pressured the consumers, who are now in open revolt against that regime.*
[1911, tr. J.-P. Turcotte in *Deb. House of Commons* (Canada) 21 Apr. 7516)]

Pressurize is earliest attested in 1944 with the sense 'produce or maintain pressure artificially in (a container, closed spaced, etc.)' (10):[33]

(10) *The fuselage will be pressurized so that at all altitudes cabin conditions will be equivalent to a height of 8,000 ft.*
[1944, *Aeronautics* Sept. 56/2]

However, at some point, both forms overlap and attestations of *pressure* used to refer to physical pressure ('apply physical pressure to, to press, pressurize') are first found in 1961 in an entry of the *Webster's Third New International Dictionary of the English Language* (11) and in 1979 in an extract from the *Daily Telegraph* (12):

(11) *Pressure, to increase or intensify pressure in; pressurize.*
[1961, Webster's 3rd New Internat. Dict. Eng. Lang.]

33 The OED provides an earlier attestation from 1940 of the *-ing* adjectival form:
The pressurizing mechanism maintains ideal weather within this passenger chamber.
[*Freeport* (Illinois) *Jrnl. Standard* 19 Mar. 2/3, 1940].

(12) *The engine on the right would have continued to pressure the No. 3 [hydraulic] system under normal circumstances.*
[1979, *Daily Tel.* 8 June 2/1]

In turn, attestations of *pressurize* in the sense 'subject to moral, psychological, or other non-physical pressure' date back to 1945 in the newspaper *Lima News* (13):

(13) *Thus, selective service continues to 'pressurize' recalcitrant military unfits into war plants.*
[1945, *Lima* (Ohio) *News* 17 Jan. 3/1]

Fig. 23 shows the competition between *pressure* and *pressurize* for the physical and non-physical senses:

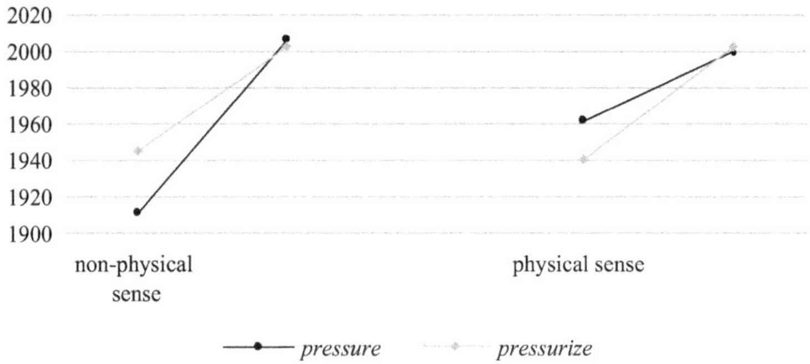

Fig. 23. Timelines for the physical and non-physical senses of *pressure/pressurize* (minimum Y-axis value is set at 1900 for easier reading)

A note of caution is in order here: the third version of the OED lists the senses by attestation date. As Allan (2012: 36) points out, chronological order '[…] cannot be taken to represent the actual chronological sequence of sense development'. However, as she continues, '[d]erivationally related lexemes might shed light on the most likely sense development'. A look at the paradigms in which the competing verbs are allocated shows that related forms seem to support this development.

Both *pressurization* and *pressurized* are attested slightly earlier than *pressurize* in the sense related to physical force. Instances of *pressurized* in the figurative sense are earliest attested in 1953, while *pressurization* and *pressurizer* are only attested in the physical sense. *Pressured* is earliest recorded with the sense 'stressful, urgent, pressing' in 1868 and as a synonym for *pressurized* in the physical sense in 1902, close to the earliest attestation of *pressure* (1911). Therefore, it is unclear whether the physical sense in the adjectival form may not be an extension of the earliest sense attested, i.e., 'stressful, urgent, pressing'. The aim here is not to draw the exact chronological development of the competitors and their paradigms, but to show that they may be used as evidence to support the semantic development of the competitors as described in the dictionary. In any case, the two forms are apparently in use in both the physical and non-physical sense according to the OED.

The competition between both verbs is also attested in contemporary dictionaries: *pressure* is defined as a synonym for *pressurize* in both *Collins* and *Merriam-Webster*. Regarding corpus evidence, both *pressure* and *pressurize* are recorded in corpora (Tab. 36), even if the converted form is recorded with a higher frequency:

Tab. 36. Corpus data for *pressure* and *pressurize*

	EHCB		**COHA**		**COCA**	
pressure	33	0.03	640	1.58	5846	5.89
pressurize	0	0	72	0.18	497	0.5

In this particular case, the use of collocates in the COCA provides information on the competition between both forms. As shown in Tabs. 37 and 38, *pressure* is most commonly attested with words such as *felt, congress, sex* or *companies*, as opposed to *pressurize*, for which their collocates reveal prevalence of the physical sense (*gas, fuel, water* or *cabin*). Thus, it seems that, while *pressure* prevails with the sense 'apply moral force', *pressurize* is apparently more common in technical domains.

Tab. 37. Comparison of the collocates in the COCA for *pressure* (W1) and *pressurize* (W2)

Word	W1	W2	W1/W2	Score
FELT	170	0	340.0	28.9
PRESIDENT	147	0	294.0	25.0
ME	292	1	292.0	24.8
HIM	468	2	234.0	19.9
NEVER	85	0	170.0	14.5
CONGRESS	79	0	158.0	13.4
STATES	76	0	152.0	12.9
SHOULD	73	0	146.0	12.4
STOP	70	0	140.0	11.9
ISRAEL	68	0	136.0	11.6
SEX	66	0	132.0	11.2
PARENTS	65	0	130.0	11.1
FEELING	64	0	128.0	10.9
COMPANIES	62	0	124.0	10.5
CHANGE	61	0	122.0	10.4
U.S.	61	0	122.0	10.4
ADMINISTRATION	60	0	120.0	10.2

Tab. 38. Comparison of collocates in the COCA for *pressurize* (W1) and *pressure* (W2)

Word	W2	W1	W2/W1	Score
GAS	19	0	38.0	447.0
FUEL	17	0	34.0	399.9
WATER	32	1	32.0	376.4
CABIN	21	1	21.0	247.0
TANKS	21	1	21.0	247.0
SUIT	18	1	18.0	211.7
CAPSULE	8	0	16.0	188.2
HEATED	8	0	16.0	188.2
POUNDS	8	0	16.0	188.2
PSI	8	0	16.0	188.2
PUMP	14	1	14.0	164.7
GASES	7	0	14.0	164.7
LIQUID	7	0	14.0	164.7
FLUID	6	0	12.0	141.2
TUNNEL	6	0	12.0	141.2
TANK	11	1	11.0	129.4
REACTOR	5	0	10.0	117.6

This analysis of the doublet *pressure/pressurize* should be understood only as a rough description of the profile of competition researched here. A detailed account of the distribution of the forms would provide further information on whether they really qualify as competition and, in that case, if such competition is resolved or not and, in the latter case, in which direction. As Fradin (2019) claims, distribution is essential when assessing competition. However, one of the main limitations in the clusters analysed here is precisely the lack of data available for a comparison of their distribution. As mentioned above, the little data available for some of the forms may also be illustrative of their low frequency, which again may indicate that competition between forms with the same base is less common than previously thought, as argued by Plag (1999) and against Gottfurcht (2008).

5.2.4.3.4 Unresolved competition: factor/factorize and fluoridate/fluoridize

In other cases, competition may extend to the rest of the members of the paradigm as well. For example, in the cluster, *factor/factorize*, the derivatives *factorable* and *factorizable* ('expressible as a product of factors') are recorded in the OED as synonyms, as well as *factoring* and *factorizing* ('the action of process of resolving a quantity into factors, or expressing it as a product or factors').

Similarly, the verbs *fluoridate* and *fluoridize* are both recorded to be in use with the sense 'add fluoride to drinking water, toothpaste, in order to prevent or reduce tooth decay' in the OED, as well as the related forms *fluoridation/fluoridization* and *fluoridated/fluoridized.*

5.3 Competition in affixation

This section addresses the competition in doublets where both competitors are derived through affixation and which amount to 47 doublets. Specifically, the competition between *-ize* suffixation vs *-ate* suffixation (e.g., *myelinize/myelinate* 'enclose a nerve fibre or fibres in myelin') amounts to 21 doublets, for which the following six semantic categories are identified:

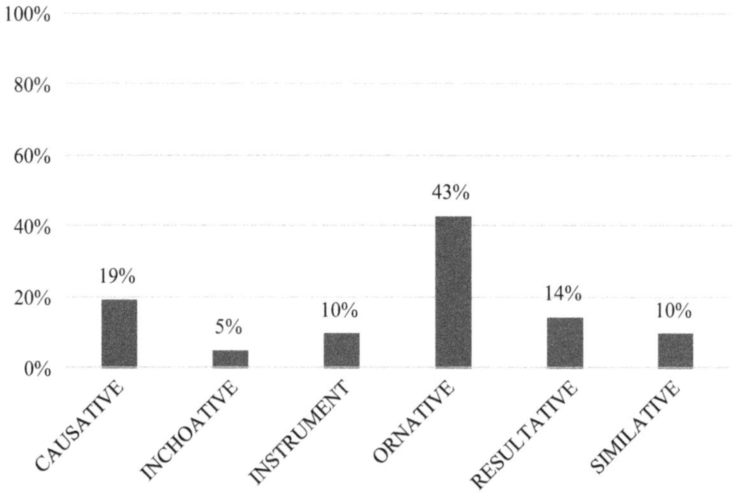

Fig. 24. The semantic distribution of doublets of competition between *-ize* suffixation and *-ate* suffixation

Fig. 24 shows that:

i) Nine doublets, i.e., 29 %, express the category ORNATIVE.
ii) Four doublets, i.e., 19 %, express the category CAUSATIVE.
iii) Three doublets, i.e., 14 %, express the category INSTRUMENT.
iv) Three doublets, i.e., 14 %, express the category RESULTATIVE.
v) Two doublets, i.e., 10 %, express the category SIMILATIVE.
vi) One doublet, i.e., 5 %, expresses the category INCHOATIVE.

As regards the profile of competition in doublets of competition between *-ize* suffixation and *-ate* suffixation:

i) Twelve doublets, i.e., 57 %, show resolved competition (e.g., *pendulate/pendulize* 'dangle, sway to and fro').
ii) Six doublets, i.e., 19 %, show ongoing competition (e.g., *oxygenate/oxygenize* 'supply or mix a substance with oxygen').
iii) Three doublets, i.e., 14 %, show past competition (e.g., *pedestrianate/pedestrianize* 'act as a pedestrian').

The competition between *-ize* suffixation and *-ify* suffixation (e.g., *etherify/etherize* 'convert into an ether') amounts to 26 doublets, i.e., 55 %, for which the following five semantic categories are identified (Fig. 25):

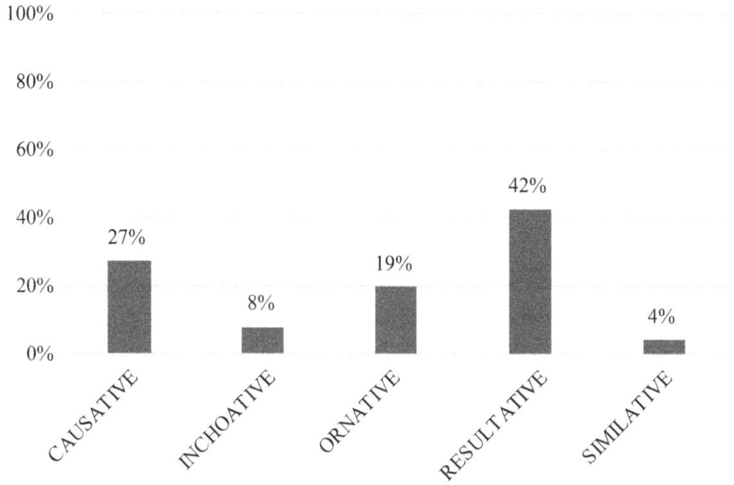

Fig. 25. The semantic distribution of doublets of competition between -*ize* suffixation and -*ify* suffixation

Fig. 25 shows that:

i) Twelve doublets, i.e., 46 %, express the category RESULTATIVE.
ii) Seven doublets, i.e., 27 %, express the category CAUSATIVE.
iii) Five doublets, i.e., 19 %, express the category ORNATIVE.
iv) Two doublets, i.e., 8 %, express the category INCHOATIVE.
v) One doublet, i.e., 4 %, expresses the category SIMILATIVE.

Regarding the profile of resolution of competition in doublets of competition between -*ize* suffixation and -*ify* suffixation:

i) Fifteen doublets, i.e., 58 %, show resolved competition (e.g., *resinify*/*resinize* 'convert into resin').
ii) Eight doublets, i.e., 31 %, show ongoing competition (e.g., *rigidify*/*rigidize* 'make a material rigid').
iii) Three doublets, i.e., 12 %, show past competition (e.g., *pyritify*/*pyritize* 'impregnate with pyrites').

The results obtained from the comparison of the 319 doublets extracted from the OED evidence the heterogeneity of competition regarding formal and semantic aspects.

Regarding the form, doublets have been divided into two groups according to their competition patterns: overt vs covert affixation (273 doublets) and competition in overt affixation (47 doublets). The patterns with the highest number of forms in competition recorded in the dictionary are conversion vs *-ize* suffixation (129 doublets) and conversion vs *-en* suffixation (70 doublets).

Regarding the meaning, competition is attested in twelve semantic categories in overt vs covert affixation, and in six categories in the competition in overt affixation. The study of competition according to senses and its classification into semantic categories allows to draw a distinction in the forms preferred for the resolution of competition. Specifically, regarding the competition between conversion and affixation, the former prevails for the expression of the categories ORNATIVE and PERFORMATIVE, while the latter prevails in the categories CAUSATIVE and INCHOATIVE.

5.4 Summary

This chapter presents the main findings in the competition of the verbal doublets analysed. Overall, the results point out to a marked heterogeneity of the phenomenon, regarding the forms and semantic categories involved, the individual peculiarities of some clusters, and the limitations inherent to the use of dictionary and corpora.

Regarding the number of competitors, the results obtained suggest that competition is more likely to involve two competitors (319 doublets), while clusters with three or more forms are much less numerous (31 clusters). Of the 350 clusters analysed, competition among more than three forms is attested in only one cluster (*fossil/fossilate/fossilify/fossilize*).

Regarding the form, the competition between conversion and *-ize* suffixation amounts to the highest number of clusters (129 doublets out of 319 doublets), followed by the competition between conversion and *-en* suffixation (70 doublets out of 319 doublets).

Regarding semantic classification, clusters are distributed across 12 semantic categories, of which CAUSATIVE, ORNATIVE and RESULTATIVE amount to 63 % of the total number of the clusters analysed. It is important to highlight that semantic classification has been made at the level of the sense, not the lexeme, as it is crucial for the assessment of competition to identify the particular senses in which two or more forms may overlap. This is especially relevant if we consider that competition between monosemous verbs is attested in only 32 clusters, thus indicating that in most cases clusters contain at least a polysemous verb for which competition occurs at a specific sense.

Whether meaning influenced the direction of the resolution of competition or not is unclear. The results obtained for the competition between conversion and affixation seem to indicate that CAUSATIVE and INCHOATIVE categories show a bias towards affixation, while the success of conversion is more common in other categories such as ORNATIVE and PERFORMATIVE. However, the low number of clusters identified for some of the categories prevents any attempt at generalization.

With respect to the profile of competition, 171 clusters displayed resolved competition, while those in which all the competitors are attested to be in use according to the OED amount to 112 clusters. Therefore, the results are in line with previous research in that competition is always expected to reach an end (Aronoff 2016).

Methodologically, despite the fact that the OED proves to be a valuable source for data collection, the heterogeneity displayed by the clusters analysed and the limitations inherent in historical research requires the combination of several resources in order to assess competition. In particular, historical and contemporary corpora, contemporary dictionaries and derivational paradigms may provide further information on the resolution of competition in some of the clusters described for illustration. In other cases, conversely, the lack of available data makes it impossible to draw conclusions on the profile of competition.

Conclusions

Despite the growing interest in morphological competition in the past years, the competition between forms with the same base has received comparatively much less attention.

Studies addressing the competition of forms with the same base and meaning are usually restricted to the comparison of two competitors, e.g., *-ity*/*-ness* (Riddle 1985), *-ic*/*-ical* (Kaunisto 2007), zero-affixation/*-ation* (Lara-Clares 2017), *-able*/*-some* (Smith 2020). In the case of competition in verbal derivation, research on doublets has been limited to the patterns of conversion vs *-en* suffixation (Bauer et al. 2010), *-ify* suffixation vs *-ize* suffixation (Lindsay 2012; Lindsay & Aronoff 2013) and conversion vs *-ize* suffixation (Fernández-Alcaina 2017; Fernández-Alcaina & Čermák 2018).

Regarding the interaction between competition and derivational paradigms, previous research has suggested that they play a role (Fernández-Alcaina & Čermák 2018; Fradin 2019: 87), although this may go unnoticed due to the 'profusion of constructs in attested families' (Fradin 2019: 87). This is especially difficult in diachronic competition.

The results obtained provide further quantitative evidence for the need of assessing competition by sense. Specifically, the initial list of 264 groups of verbs where competition is attested in at least one of their senses has been expanded up to 350 clusters. This is especially relevant for doublets where the distinction of clusters according to sense allows the identification of 319 doublets out of the 237 pairs extracted from the OED. This highlights the need for assessing competition by sense and is in line with methodological decisions in previous research on competition (e.g., Díaz-Negrillo 2017; Fernández-Domínguez 2017; Fradin 2019; Smith 2020).

As mentioned above, the profile of competition is highly heterogeneous as regards both the competing patterns and the semantic categories involved.

In the case of doublets, this study identifies eight patterns of competition, of which 42 % of the groups represent the competition between conversion and *-ize* suffixation (100 pairs). In fact, both conversion and *-ize* suffixation are the two processes with the highest number of attestations in the groups of competitors identified: conversion appears in 206 of the 264 groups (78 %), while *-ize* suffixation appears in 171 groups (65 %).

The amount of actual morphological competition may be distorted by OED data: they may provide an inordinate picture of the actual import of competition. Specifically, the attestation of clusters where one of the forms is attested only once in the OED raises questions on the real extent to which competition occurs in the language, since they seem to be rather the results of individual innovations that did not seem to extend to the rest of the community.

In turn, corpus data can lead to an underrepresentation of competition because there are no records for many of the forms analysed. While this prevents any further analysis of the use of the competitors, it may also be considered evidence of the low frequency of cases of competition.

Another point that may be illustrative of the marginality of competition is the variety of profiles displayed by the clusters analysed regarding various aspects.

Regarding the number of competitors per cluster, of the 350 clusters identified, 319 contain two forms, 30 clusters have three members, and competition among more than three forms is only attested in one cluster. However, even in those cases where there are three forms competing for the same meaning, competition is usually reduced to two forms, as shown by the clusters displaying 'partial competition'.

As regards the degree of overlap of senses, competition is usually attested in one specific sense, even if some clusters, e.g., *black/blacken* or *character/characterize*, present almost complete competition across their senses. The varying degrees of overlap between competitors also raise questions on whether it is possible to encompass all the phenomena described as instances of competition.

Although the clusters collected represent fifteen different patterns of competition, conversion and *-ize* suffixation are the two most common competitors. This was to be expected, since both are, allegedly, the two most productive processes of verb formation in English. At the same time, this may also be indicative of the nature of competition: the higher the productivity, the more likely it is for a verb to find a competitor. Different periods can have different productive processes, and this explains the high number of doublets of competition between conversion and *-en* suffixation identified in this work, even if the latter is considered to be no longer productive.

Despite the heterogeneity of competition, resolution is always the most common outcome independently of the number of competitors, the degree of overlap, the patterns in competition and the meaning expressed. However, it can also display various profiles. For example, competition in some clusters may be resolved following a pattern:

i) *-ize* suffixation prevails in a number of triplets, independently of the rest of competitors.
ii) *-ize* suffixation prevails over conversion in CAUSATIVE doublets.
iii) There is a general replacement of conversion by *-en* suffixation in CAUSATIVE and INCHOATIVE doublets. In turn, conversion prevails over *-en* suffixation in non-CAUSATIVE senses.

In other cases, resolution depends on specific clusters. This may be due to the influence of borrowing (e.g., *personify/personate/personize*), the existence of semantically related forms (e.g., *passivate/passivify/passivate*) or simply because there is no longer a need (e.g., *margin/marginate*).

Resolution may be achieved by the obsolescence of the competing sense in one of the forms, which is the most common profile in the clusters analysed. This may be partly a result of the inclusion of rare words in the OED, usually coined as synonyms for well-established forms.

In other cases, both competitors are apparently in use in Present-Day English but with differentiated meanings (e.g., *pressure/pressurize*). This is attested to a lesser extent in the clusters analysed, possibly as the result of an underrepresentation of specialized domains in the OED. This is of course expected given the impossibility of providing a full coverage of the language. Limitations of this type emphasize the complexity of research on competition.

All in all, competition between patterns in verbs with the same base is rare as shown by the low number of clusters analysed. Even within such a complex morphological model as the one in English, where the original Germanic morphology model coexists with the eventually superseding Romance morphology model, the language system proves that it is the economical system that it is supposed to be. This is particularly remarkable in two further respects: it is economical to a surprisingly high degree of efficiency, and by the operation of a number of rules that may be governed by one of the competing forms, by the semantic category expressed or that can be lexically-governed (rather than by a general principle).

Methodologically, this study has also highlighted some implications that need to be considered in future research. The heterogeneity and the apparently low frequency of the phenomena described here pose a number of methodological challenges to an account of the profile of competition. In some cases, the lack of available data impedes drawing any conclusions.

The OED has proved to be a useful tool for the collection and description of verbal competitors, but the limitations inherent in the use of lexicographic resources makes it necessary to use it in combination with other dictionaries and with both historical and synchronic corpora. Ideally, the assessment of the competition of two forms should take into account the distribution of the forms (Fradin 2019). In the study of diachronic competition, however, this is in most cases unattainable: most of the clusters identified here have one or none of their forms recorded in corpora, thus making impossible any further analysis in this respect.

In view of the lack of available data and based on previous research (Fernández-Alcaina & Čermák 2018), this study has analysed the competition of verbal clusters considering the paradigms where they are allocated. The derivational family has been considered as a factor playing a role in the competition of doublets (Fradin 2019). In fact, the inclusion of related forms has contributed to shed light on the competition in certain clusters (e.g., *pillory/pillorize*). Conversely, in other cases, partly due to the lack of data (e.g., *heaven/heavenize*) and partly due to the difficulties stemming from historical research, derivational paradigms have not provided any information.

Specifically, the analysis of related forms can contribute to the study of verbal competition in various ways:

i) by supporting the current prevalence of one of the competitors, when both are recorded as in use in the OED (e.g., *pillory/pillorize*, *revolution/revolutionize*),
ii) by specifying whether semantic specialization exists (e.g., *pressure/pressurize*), and
iii) by providing evidence on the extension of ongoing competition to other members of the paradigm (e.g., *fluoridate/fluoridize*).

Another methodological limitation is the restriction in the choice of the competitors to those formed by conversion and affixation. In fact, previous research on competition in forms with the same base is usually restricted to the analysis of the competition of two specific affixes (e.g., Kaunisto 2007, 2009; Baeskow 2012; Lindsay & Aronoff 2013; Fernández-Alcaina 2017; Lara-Clares 2017; Lara-Clares & Thompson 2019; Smith 2020). Although the choice allows for a delimited sample, the restriction to specific processes may lead in many cases to misleading conclusions on the status and competition of the forms. In particular, the resolution of competition in some of the clusters may be explained by the existence of a third (or fourth form, in the case of triplets) with a different base. Thus, in the triplet *perfection/perfectionate/perfectionize*, the existence of the well-established verb *perfect* with the sense 'make perfect' would explain why the three forms are marked as 'rare' in the OED

It must be noted, however, that the study of diachronic competition cannot escape from the limitations inherent in the use of lexicographic and corpus resources and, from a wider perspective, in historical linguistics. Therefore, it should be admitted that the profile and resolution of competition in some of the clusters identified in this study would remain unclear due to the lack of supporting evidence.

The findings of the research shed light on the features of the profile and resolution of morphological competition in verbs. They also provide evidence on the need to assess competition as part of a broader phenomenon.

References

Allan, Kathryn. 2012. Using *OED* data as evidence for researching semantic change. In Kathryn Allan & Justyna A. Robinson (eds.), *Current methods in historical semantics*, 17–40. Berlin/Boston: De Gruyter Mouton.

Amutio-Palacios, Silvia. 2013. Suffix competition in Old English word formation. *Revista Electrónica de Lingüística Aplicada* 12, 45–62.

Anderson, Stephen R. 1969. *West Scandinavian system vowels and the ordering of phonological rules.* PhD Dissertation. MIT.

Anshen, Frank & Mark Aronoff. 1999. Using dictionaries to study the mental lexicon. *Brain and Language* 68, 16–26.

Arndt-Lappe, Sabine. 2014. Analogy in suffix rivalry: the case of English *-ity* and *-ness*. *English Language & Linguistics* 18(3), 497–548.

Aronoff, Mark. 1976. *Word-formation in generative grammar.* Cambridge, MA: MIT Press.

Aronoff, Mark. 2016. Competition and the lexicon. In Annibale Elia, Claudio Iacobini & Miriam Voghera (eds.), *Livelli di Analisi e fenomeni di interfaccia. Atti del XLVII congresso internazionale della società di linguistica Italiana*, 39–52. Roma: Bulzoni Editore.

Aronoff, Mark. 2019. Competition and alternants in linguistic morphology. In Franz Rainer, Francesco Gardani, Wolfgang U. Dressler & Hans Christian Luschützky (eds.), *Competition in inflection and word-formation*, 39–66. Dordrecht: Springer.

ATILF (Université de Lorraine, CNRS) & CLLE (Université de Toulouse, CNRS). 2017. *ParadigMo. First Workshop on Paradigmatic Word Formation Modeling*, 19–20 June 2017, Toulouse (France).

Baayen, Harald. 2009. Corpus Linguistics in Morphology: morphological productivity. In Anke Lüdeling & Merja Kytö (eds.), *Corpus linguistics: An international handbook*, 899–919. Berlin/Boston: Mouton de Gruyter.

Baeskow, Heike. 2012. *-Ness* and *-ity*: phonological exponents of *n* or meaningful nominalizer of different adjectival domains? *Journal of English Linguistics* 40(1), 6–40.

Bauer, Laurie. 1983. *English word-formation.* Cambridge: Cambridge University Press.

Bauer, Laurie. 1997. Derivational paradigms. In Geert Booij & Jaap van Marle (eds.), *Yearbook of Morphology 1996*, 243–256. Dordrecht: Kluwer.

Bauer, Laurie. 2001. *Morphological productivity*. Cambridge: Cambridge University Press.

Bauer, Laurie. 2006. Competition in English word-formation. In Ans van Kemenade & Bettelou Los (eds.), *The handbook of the history of English*, 177–198. Malden, MA: Blackwell.

Bauer, Laurie. 2014. *'What is the plural of mouse?' and other unhelpful questions for morphologists*. Plenary lecture delivered at the *47th Annual Meeting of the Societas Linguistica Europaea*, 11th–14th September 2014, Poznań (Poland).

Bauer, Laurie, Rochelle Lieber & Ingo Plag. 2013. *The Oxford guide to English morphology*. Oxford: Oxford University Press.

Bauer, Laurie & Rodney Huddleston. 2002. Lexical word-formation. In Rodney Huddleston & Geoffrey K. Pullum (eds.), *The Cambridge grammar of the English language*, 1621–1721. Cambridge: Cambridge University Press.

Bauer, Laurie & Paul Nation. 1993. Word families. *International Journal of Lexicography* 6(4), 253–279.

Bauer, Laurie & Salvador Valera. 2015. Sense inheritance in English word-formation. In Laurie Bauer, Lívia Körtvelyéssy & Pavol Štekauer (eds.), *Semantics of complex words*, 67–84. Dordrecht: Springer.

Bauer, Laurie, Salvador Valera & Ana Díaz-Negrillo. 2010. Affixation vs conversion: the resolution of conflicting patterns. In Franz Rainer, Wolfgang U. Dressler, Dieter Kastovsky & Hans Christian Luschützky (eds.), *Variation and change in morphology: selected papers from the 13th International Morphology Meeting, Vienna, February 2008*, 15–32. Dordrecht: John Benjamins.

Beecher, Henry. 2004. *Derivational paradigm in word formation* (http://citeseerx.ist.psu.edu/viewdoc/summary?doi=10.1.1.94.9071) (Accessed 2021-04-05).

Benveniste, Émile. 1948. *Noms d'agent et noms d'action en Indo-Européen*. Paris: Adrien-Maisonneuve.

Blevins, James P. 2013. Word-based morphology from Aristotle to Modern WP (Word and Paradigm Models). In Keith Allan (ed.), *The Oxford handbook of the history of linguistics*. Oxford: Oxford University Press.

Bonami, Olivier & Jana Strnadová. 2019. Paradigm structure and predictability in derivational morphology. *Morphology* 29(2), 167–197.

Boyé, Gilles & Gauvain Schalchli. 2016. The status of paradigms. In Andrew Hippisley & Gregory Stump (eds.), *The Cambridge handbook of morphology*, 206–234. Cambridge: Cambridge University Press.

Bréal, Michel. 1897. *Essai de sémantique* (Science des significations). Paris: Hachette.

Campbell, Lyle. 2002. The history of linguistics. In Mark Aronoff & Janie Rees-Miller (eds.), *The handbook of linguistics*, 81–104. Malden, MA: Blackwell.

Carstairs-McCarthy, Andrew. 1994. Inflectional classes, gender, and the principle of contrast. *Language* 70, 737–788.

Collins. 2021. Available online at https://www.collinsdictionary.com/es/ (Accessed 2021-04-07).

Corbett, Greville G. 2010. Canonical derivational morphology. *Word Structure* 3(2), 141–155.

Corbin, Danielle. 1987. *Morphologie dérivationelle et structuration du lexique*. Tübingen: Max Niemeyer.

Coseriu, Eugenio. 1967 [1952]. Sistema, norma y habla. Reprinted in *Teoría del lenguaje y lingüística general*, 11–113. Madrid: Gredos.

Davies, Mark. 2004. *British National Corpus* (from Oxford University Press). Available online at https://www.english-corpora.org/bnc/ (Accessed 2021-04-06).

Davies, Mark. 2008–. *The Corpus of Contemporary American English (COCA)*. Available online at https://www.english-corpora.org/coca/ (Accessed 2021-04-06).

Davies, Mark. 2010. *The Corpus of Historical American (COHA)*. Available online at https://www.english-corpora.org/coha/ (Accessed 2021-04-06).

Davies, Mark. 2018. *The iWeb Corpus*. Available online at https://www.english-corpora.org/iweb/ (Accessed 2021-04-06).

Davies, Mark & Don Chapman. 2016. The effect of representativeness and size in historical corpora: an empirical study of changes in lexical frequency. In Don Chapman, Colette Moore & Miranda Wilcox (eds.), *Studies in the history of the English language VII: generalizing vs. particularizing methodologies in historical linguistic analysis*, 131–150. Berlin: De Gruyter Mouton.

Deo, Ashwini. 2007. Derivational morphology in Inheritance-Based Lexica: Insights from Pāṇini. *Lingua* 117(1), 175–201.

Department of British and American Studies (Pavol Jozef Šafárik University in Košice). 2018. *Word-Formation Theories III & Typology and Universals in Word-Formation IV*, 27–30 June 2018, Košice (Slovakia).

Department of British and American Studies (Pavol Jozef Šafárik University in Košice). 2022. *Word-Formation Theories III & Typology and Universals in Word-Formation V*, 23–26 June 2022, Košice (Slovakia).

Díaz-Negrillo, Ana. 2017. On the identification of competition in English derivational morphemes. The case of *-dom*, *-hood* and *-ship*. In Juan Santana-Lario

& Salvador Valera (eds.), *Competing patterns in English affixation*, 119–162. Bern: Peter Lang.

Early English Books Online (EEBO) Accessed via https://www.korpus.cz (Accessed 2018-11-14)

English Dictionary, Thesaurus, & Grammar Help | Lexico.com. 2021. *Lexico Dictionaries English*. Available online at https://www.lexico.com/en (Accessed 2021-04-06).

English Historical Books Collection (EHBC). Accessed via http://sketchengine.eu (Accessed 2021-04-06).

Fernández-Alcaina, Cristina. 2017. Availability and unavailability in English word-formation. In Juan Santana-Lario & Salvador Valera (eds.), *Competing patterns in English affixation*, 163–206. Bern: Peter Lang.

Fernández-Alcaina, Cristina & Jan Čermák. 2018. Derivational paradigms and competition in English: a diachronic study on competing causative verbs and their derivatives. *SKASE Journal of Theoretical Linguistics* 15(3), 69–97.

Fernández-Domínguez, Jesús. 2017. Methodological and procedural issues in the quantification of morphological competition. In Juan Santana-Lario & Salvador Valera (eds.), *Competing patterns in English affixation*, 67–118. Bern: Peter Lang.

Fernández-Domínguez, Jesús, Alexandra Bagasheva & Cristina Lara-Clares (eds.). 2020. *Paradigmatic relations in word formation*. Leiden: Brill.

Fowler, Henry V. 1928. *A dictionary of Modern English usage*. Oxford: Clarendon Press.

Fradin, Bernard. 2019. Competition in derivation: what can we learn from French doublets in *-age* and *-ment*? In Franz Rainer, Francesco Gardani, Wolfgang U. Dressler & Hans Christian Luschützky (eds.), *Competition in inflection and word-formation*, 67–93. Dordrecht: Springer.

Gaeta, Livio & Davide Ricca. 2015. Productivity. In Peter O. Müller, Ingeborg Ohnheiser, Susan Olsen & Franz Rainer (eds.), *Word-formation: an international handbook of the languages of Europe Vol. 2*, 842–858. Berlin: De Gruyter.

Gardani, Francesco, Franz Rainer & Hans Christian Luschützky. 2019. Competition in morphology: a historical outline. In Franz Rainer, Francesco Gardani, Wolfgang U. Dressler & Hans Christian Luschützky (eds.), *Competition in inflection and word-formation*, 3–36. Dordrecht: Springer.

Gause, George F. 1934. *The struggle for existence*. Baltimore, MD: Williams & Wilkins.

Gawełko, Marek. 1977. *Evolution der suffixes adjectivaux en français*. Wrocław: Akademia Nauk.

Gottfurcht, Carolyn A. 2008. *Denominal verb formation in English*. PhD Dissertation. Northwestern University.

Gussmann, Edmund. 1987. The lexicon of English de-adjectival verbs. In Edmund Gussmann (ed.), *Rules and the lexicon*, 79–101. Lublin: Catholic University.

Harder, Peter. 1996. Linguistic structure in a functional grammar. In Elisabeth Engberg-Pedersen, Michael Fortescue, Peter Harder, Lars Heltoft & Lisbeth Falster Jakobsen (eds.), *Content, expression and structure: studies in Danish functional grammar*, 423–454. Amsterdam: John Benjamins.

Hathout, Nabil & Fiammetta Namer. 2018. Defining paradigms in word formation: concepts, data and experiments. *Lingue e linguaggio* 17(2), 151–154.

Hathout, Nabil & Fiammetta Namer. 2019. Paradigms in word formation: what are we up to? *Morphology* 29(2), 153–165.

Kastovsky, Dieter. 2005. Conversion and/or zero: word-formation theory, historical linguistics, and typology. In Laurie Bauer & Salvador Valera (eds.), *Approaches to conversion/zero-derivation*, 31–50. Münster: Waxmann.

Kaunisto, Mark. 2007. *Variation and change in the lexicon: a corpus-based analysis of adjectives in English ending in* -ic *and* -ical. Amsterdam: Rodopi.

Kaunisto, Mark. 2009. The rivalry between English adjectives ending in *-ive* and *-ory*. In Roderick W. McConchie, Alpo Honkapohja & Jukka Tyrkkö (eds.), *Selected Proceedings of the 2008 Symposium on New Approaches in English Historical Lexis*, 74–87. Somerville, MA: Cascadilla Proceedings Project.

Kiparsky, Paul. 1973. "Elsewhere" in Phonology. In Stephen R. Anderson & Paul Kiparsky (eds.), *A Festschrift for Morris Halle*, 93–106. New York, NY: Harper & Row.

Kjellmer, Göran. 2001. Why *weaken* but not **strongen*? On deadjectival verbs. *English Studies* 82, 154–171.

Körtvélyessy, Lívia, Alexandra Bagasheva, Pavol Štekauer & Salvador Valera. 2020. Introduction. In Lívia Körtvélyessy, Alexandra Bagasheva & Pavol Štekauer (eds.), *Derivational networks across languages*, 1–26. Berlin: De Gruyter Mouton.

Kroch, Anthony, Beatrice Santorini & Lauren Delfs. 2004. *The Penn-Helsinki Parsed Corpus of Early Modern English (PPCEME)*. Accessed via https://kontext.korpus.cz/ (Accessed 2018-11-14).

Lara-Clares, Cristina. 2017. Competition in Present-Day English nominalization by zero-affixation vs *-ation*. In Juan Santana-Lario & Salvador Valera (eds.), *Competing patterns in English affixation*, 207–244. Bern: Peter Lang.

Lara-Clares, Cristina & Alicia Lara-Clares. 2016. An online tool for big data sampling in research on competition in English word-formation. Paper presented at the *4th Meeting Linguistics Beyond and Within – International Linguistics Conference*, 20th–21st October 2016, Lublin (Poland).

Lara-Clares, Cristina & Paul Thompson. 2019. Nominal competition in Present-Day English affixation: zero-affixation vs *-ness* with the meaning STATIVE. *SKASE Journal of Theoretical Linguistics* 16(2), 25–50.

Lindsay, Mark. 2012. Rival suffixes: synonymy, competition, and the emergence of productivity. In Angela Ralli, Geert Booij, Sergio Scalise & Athanasios Karasimos (eds.), *Proceedings of the 8th Mediterranean Morphology Meeting – Morphology and the Architecture of Grammar*, 192–203. Patras: University of Patras.

Lindsay, Mark & Mark Aronoff. 2013. Natural selection in self-organizing morphological systems. In Fabio Montermini, Gilles Boyé & Jesse Tseng (eds.), *Morphology in Toulouse: Selected Proceedings of Décembrettes 7*, 133–153. Munich: Lincom Europe.

MacWhinney, Brian, Andrej Malchukov & Edith Moravcsik (eds.). 2014. *Competing motivations in grammar and usage*. Oxford: Oxford University Press.

Mal'ceva, I. M. 1966. Iz nabljudenij nad slovoobrazovaniem v jazyke XVIII. Veka (na materiale odnokorennyx parallelej *-ost\-stvo*, I *-ost\-ie*) [From observations of word-formation in the language of the 18th century (based on material of same-based parallels *-ost'*, *-stvo*, and *-ost'*, *-ie*)]. In Jurij S. Sorokin (ed.), *Processy formirovanija leksiki russkogo literaturnogo jazyka* [The processes of formation of the lexicon of the Russian literary language], 259–264. Moscow: Nauka.

Marchand, Hans. 1969. *The categories and types of Present-Day English word formation. A synchronic-diachronic approach*. Munich: Carl Beck.

Merriam-Webster. 2021. Available online at https://www.merriam-webster.com (Accessed 2021-04-06).

Moravcsik, Edith. 2014. Introduction. In Brian MacWhinney, Andrej Malchukov & Edith Moravcsik (eds.), *Competing motivations in grammar and usage*, 1–14. Oxford: Oxford University Press.

Nevalainen, Terttu. 1999. Early Modern English lexis and semantics. In Roger Lass (ed.), *The Cambridge history of the English language Vol. 3, 1476–1776*, 332–458. Cambridge: Cambridge University Press.

Nielsen, Peter Juul. 2016. *Functional structure in morphology and the case of non-finite verbs: theoretical issues and the description of the Danish verb system*. Leiden: Brill.

Plag, Ingo. 1999. *Morphological productivity: structural constraints on English derivation*. Berlin/New York: Mouton de Gruyter.

Plag, Ingo. 2000. On the mechanisms of morphological rivalry: a new look at competing verb-deriving affixes in English. In Bernhard Reitz & Sigrid Rieuwerts (eds.), *Anglistentag 1999 Mainz Proceedings*, 63–76. Trier: WVT.

Plank, Frans. 1981. *Morphologische (Ir-)Regularitäten*. Tübingen: Narr.

Pounder, Amanda. 2000. *Processes and paradigms in word-formation morphology*. Berlin/Hawthorne, NY: Mouton de Gruyter.

Prince, Alan & Paul Smolensky. 1993. *Optimality theory*. Ms. Rutgers University.

Proffitt, Michael. 2021. *The Oxford English Dictionary*. Available online at http://www.oed.com (Accessed 2021-04-06).

Quirk, Randolph, Geoffrey Leech, Sydney Greenbaum & Jan Svartvik. 1985. *A comprehensive grammar of the English language*. London: Longman.

Rainer, Franz. 1988. Towards a theory of blocking: the case of Italian and German quality nouns. In Geert Booij & Jaap van Marle (eds.), *Yearbook of morphology*, 155–185. Dordrecht: Foris.

Rainer, Franz. 1993. *Spanische Wortbildungslehre*. Tübingen: Max Niemeyer.

Rainer, Franz, Francesco Gardani & Elisabeth Peters (organizers). 2016. *17th International Morphology Meeting*, 18–21 February 2016, Vienna (Austria).

Rainer Franz, Francesco Gardani, Wolfgang U. Dressler & Hans Christian Luschützky (eds.). 2019. *Competition in inflection and word-formation*. Dordrecht: Springer.

Renner, Vincent. 2020. An ecosystem view of English word-formation. *The Mental Lexicon* 15(1), 4–20.

Riddle, Elizabeth M. 1985. A historical perspective on the productivity of the suffixes *-ness* and *-ity*. In Jacek Fisiak (ed.), *Historical semantics: historical word-formation*, 435–461. Berlin: Mouton.

Robins, Robert H. 2000. Classical antiquity. In Geert Booij, Christian Lehman & Joachim Mugdan, in collaboration with Stavros Skopeteas (eds.), *Morphology. An international handbook of inflection and word-formation Vol I*, 52–67. Berlin: Walter de Gruyter.

Roché, Michael. 2009. Pour une morphologie lexicale. *Mémoires de la Société de Linguistique de Paris*, n.s. 17, 65–87.

Roché, Michel. 2011. Quelle morphologie? In Michel Roché, Gilles Boyé, Nabil Hathout, Stéphanie Lignon & Marc Plénat (eds.), *Des unités morphologiques au lexique, langues et syntaxe*, 15–39. Plymouth: Hermes Science Publishing.

Romaine, Suzanne. 2004. Change in productivity. In Geert Booij, Christian Lehmann & Joachim Mugdan, in collaboration with Stavros Skopeteas (eds.),

Morphology. An international handbook on inflection and word-formation, 1636–1644. Berlin/New York: Mouton de Gruyter.

Santana-Lario, Juan & Salvador Valera (eds.). 2017. *Competing patterns in English affixation*. Bern: Peter Lang.

Saussure, Ferdinand de. 1959 [1916]. *Cours de linguistique générale*. New York, NY: Philosophical Press.

Scherer, Carmen. 2015. Change in productivity. In Peter O. Müller, Ingeborg Ohnheiser, Susan Olsen & Franz Rainer (eds.), *Word-formation. An international handbook of the languages of Europe Vol. 3*, 1781–1793. Berlin: De Gruyter.

Schneider, Edgar W. 1987. Beobachtungen zur Paradigmatik der verbbildenden Suffixe *-en*, *-ify* und *-ize* im Englischen. *Sprachwissenschaft* 12(1), 88–109.

Schupbach, Richard. 1984. *Lexical specialization in Russian*. Columbus: Slavica.

Simpson, John. 2004. The OED and collaborative research into the history of English. *Anglia* 122(2): 185–208.

Smith, Chris A. 2020. A case study of *-some* and *-able* derivatives in the OED3: examining the diachronic output and productivity of two competing adjectival suffixes. *Journal of English Lexicology* 16. Available online at https://journals.openedition.org/lexis/ (Accessed 2021-04-97).

Štekauer, Pavol. 2014. Derivational paradigms. In Rochelle Lieber & Pavol Štekauer (eds.), *The Oxford handbook of derivational morphology*, 354–369. Oxford: Oxford University Press.

Štekauer, Pavol. 2017. Competition in natural languages. In Juan Santana-Lario & Salvador Valera (eds.), *Competing patterns in English affixation*, 15–32. Bern: Peter Lang.

Stockwell, Robert & Donka Minkova. 2009. *English words: history and structure*. 2nd edn. Cambridge: Cambridge University Press.

Stump, Gregory. 2001. *Inflectional morphology*. Cambridge: Cambridge University Press.

Societas Linguistica Europeae. 2016. *49th Annual Meeting of the Societas Linguistica Europaea*, 31 August–3 September 2016, Naples (Italy).

Thornton, Anna-Maria. 2012. Overabundance in Italian verb morphology and its interactions with other non-canonical phenomena. In Thomas Stolz, Hitomi Otsuka & Aina Urdze (eds.), *Studia typologica: irregularity in morphology (and beyond)*, 251–269. Berlin/Boston, PA: De Gruyter.

Université Bordeaux-Montaigne. 2021. *ParadigMo 2. Paradigm-based approaches to word-formation modeling*, 3–4 June 2021, Boudeaux (France).

Valera, Salvador. 2020. Semantic patterns in noun-to-verb conversion in English. In Lívia Körtvélyessy & Pavol Štekauer (eds.), *Complex words: advance in morphology*, 311–334. Cambridge: Cambridge University Press.

van Marle, Jaap. 1985. *On the paradigmatic dimension of morphological creativity.* Dordrecht: Foris.

van Marle, Jaap. 1986. The Domain Hypothesis: the study of rival morphological processes. *Linguistics* 24, 601–627.

van Marle, Jaap. 1994. Paradigms. *Encyclopaedia of Language and Linguistics.* Oxford: Pergamon.

von Bahder, Karl. 1880. *Die Verbalabstracta in den germanischen Sprachen, ihrer Bildung nach dargestellt.* Halle: Max Niemeyer.

Wunderlich, Dieter. 2001. How gaps and substitutions can become optimal: the pronominal affix paradigms of Yimas. *Transactions of the Philological Society* 99(2), 315–366.

Appendices

Appendix 1: Competing triplets

Lemma	S	Semantic category	Timeline		Lemma	S	Semantic category	Timeline	
			*	†				*	†
carbonate2	2		1799	1831	*pauper*	-		1841	2002
carbonify	2	RES	1801	1984	*pauperize*	-	RES	1834	1992
carbonize	1		1798	2002	*pauperate*	-		1839	1839
gangrenize	-		1598/ 1860	1602/ 1978	*empatron*	-		1609/ 1904	2010
gangrenate	2	INCH	1631	2003	*patron*	-	SIM	1624	2002
gangrene	1b		1614	2005	*patronize*	1a		1593	1998
missionate	-	PERF	1815	1966	*heroify*	-	SIM	1677	1999
missionize1/2			1826	1993	*heroize*	1a		1695	2007
mission	2		1898	1898	*hero*	-		1762	1992
moist	2		1382	2000	*fossil*	-		1750	2003
moisten	2a	CAUS	1559	1989	*fossilize*	2a	RES	1794	1997
moistify	-		1786	1882	*fossilate*	-		1822	1972
					fossilify	-		1843	1969
moisten	2b		1567	1983	*French*	6		1833	2006
moistify	-	CAUS	1786	1882	*Frenchify*	1	CAUS	1592	2001
moist	4b		1530	1892	*Frenchize*	-		1849	1994
neat	1a		1575	1994	*historify*	1		1586	1986
neaten	-	CAUS	1828	2003	*historize*	1	PERF	1572	1995
neatify	-		1581	1685	*history*	1		1475	2001
personify	1		1728	1989	*parcel*	1a		1416	1989
personate	6	RES	1612/ 1823	1997	*parcellate*	-	RES	1927	1998
personize	2		1726	1846	*parcellize*	-		1606/ 1989	2003
statue2	2		1628	1941	*patine*	-		1896	2002
statufy	2	RES	1868	2006	*patinate*	-	ORN	1867	1990
statuize	-		1718	1944	*patinize*	-		1948	2001

Lemma	S	Semantic category	Timeline *	Timeline †	Lemma	S	Semantic category	Timeline *	Timeline †
god	2a		1595	1956	*English*	1a		1450	1995
godify	-	RES	1603	2012	*Englishize*	-	CAUS	1799	2006
godize	-		1592	1993	*Englify*	-		1688	2006
					Englishify	-		1855	2000
immune	-		1849	1989	*English*	3a		1711	2002
immunize	1a	CAUS	1889	2001	*Englishize*	-	CAUS	1799	2006
immunify	-		1892	1905	*Englify*	-		1688	2006
					Englishify	-		1855	2000
quiet	1		1398	2002	*structure*	1a		1664	2008
quieten	1	CAUS	1759	1998	*structurate*	-	ORN	1664/ 1927	2006
quietize	-		1791/ 1932	1997	*structurize*	-		1912	2004
immune	-		1849	1989	*substantivate*	-		1613/ 1868	2002
immunize	1a	CAUS	1889	2001	*substantivize*	-	RES	1848	2002
immunify	-		1892	1905	*substantive*			1678	1994
function	1a		1844	2009	*gangrenate*	1		1532	1992
functionate	-	PERF	1843	1961	*gangrenize*	-	CAUS	1978	1978
functionize	-		1847	1927	*gangrene*	1a		1597	1935
passivate	1		1913	1992	*perfection*	-		1651	1999
passivize	1	CAUS	1910	1983	*perfectionate*	-	CAUS	1570	1993
passivify	-		1907	1934	*perfectionize*	-		1805	1997
pollen	-		1877	1983	*storify*1	-		1616	1997
pollinate	1	ORN	1873	1994	*storize*	-	RES	1590	1594
pollinize	-		1873	1999	*story*1	1		1449	2004
enthrone	1		1543	2012					
throne	-	LOC	1390	2015					
thronize	-		1513	1711					
thrononize	-		1500	1533					
resin	-		1760	2005					
resinate	-	ORN	1891	2000					
resinize	-		1848	1912					

Appendix 2: Competing doublets

2.1 Conversion vs prefixation

Lemma	S	Semantic category	Timeline *	†	Lemma	S	Semantic category	Timeline *	†
belittle	2	CAUS	1789	2004	*empoison*	3	ORN	1596	1854
little	1a		eOE/ 1885	1696/ 2002	*poison*	1b		1582	1990
belord	2	STAT	1858	1914	*empoison*	5	INST	1400	1922
lord	4b		1563	2005	*poison*	2a		1395	1993
belimb	-	PRIV	1225/ 1831	1330/ 1983	*empowder*	-	ORN	1548	1933
limb	1a		1674	1888	*powder*1	I		1335	2005
belord	1	SIM	1565	1945	*empower*	2a	ORN	1643	2010
lord	3c		1633	1872	*power*	1		1592	1729
belord	1	ORN	1565	1945	*empride*	1	RES	1410	1652
lord	3b		1616	1889	*pride*	4		1440	1969
belord	2	STAT	1858	1914	*empurple*	1	CAUS	1590	1998
lord	2		1450	1999	*purple*	1		1475	1991
bedung	2	ORN	1649	1992	*empurple*	1	INCH	1590	1998
dung	1a		800	2017	*purple*	1		1608	1992
empacket	-	RES	1825	1917	*enjewel*	1	ORN	1611	1990
packet	1		1621	2001	*jewel*	1a		1551	2014
empanel	-	LOC	1426	2005	*empoison*	1	ORN	1374	1999
panel	1a		1451	1839	*poison*	1a		1350	1998
empeople	1	ORN	1582	1995	*empoison*	2	ORN	1450	2006
people	1a		1475	1986	*poison*	3		1470	1991
emplaster	1	INST	1400/ 1992	1712/ 1997	*empoison*	4	INST	1775	2008
plaster	1a		1398	1004	*poison*	4a		1513	1994
emplaster	2	ORN	1405/ 1649	1943	*empoison*	7	STAT	1780	1946
plaster	2		1400	2004	*poison*	2b		1450	1994
emplume	-	ORN	1611	1992	*enqueue*	-	LOC	1971	1998
plume	1a		1449	1987	*queue*	3c		1973	2004

2.2 Conversion vs *-ate* suffixation

Lemma	S	Semantic category	Timeline		Lemma	S	Semantic category	Timeline	
			*	†				*	†
culturate	-	PERF	1631	1884	*active*	-	CAUS	1620/ 1969	2005
culture	1a		1510	1999	*activate*	1a		1624	2006
faction	2	RES	1656/ 1953	1997	*motive*	1	ORN	1657	1988
factionate	2		1642/ 1970	1995	*motivate*	1a		1836	1991
margin	2b	ORN	1815	1983	*value*	1a	RES	1434	2004
marginate	2		1611/ 1880	1623/ 1979	*valuate*	-		1588	2009
motivate	2	ORN	1970	2000	*margin*	1	ORN	1595	1885
motive	2		1830	1909	*marginate*	1		1609	1609
nervate	-	ORN	1682	1792	*person*	2	ORN	1644	1644
nerve	2		1694	1968	*personate*	1		1591	1705
nitrate	-	INST	1872	1992	*passion*	1a	ORN	1467	1997
nitre	-		1880	1908	*passionate*	1		1566	1886
petition	1	RES	1607	1991	*potion*	-	INST	1611	2003
petitionate	1		1624	1633	*potionate*	-		1623	1623
petition	2	PERF	1611	1994	*affection*	-	PERF	1545	1921
petitionate	2		1625	1625	*affectionate*	1		1565	1916
alembic	-	INST	1635	1902	*notion*	2	RES	1894	1997
alembicate	-		1627	2001	*notionate*	-		1645	1660
arsenic	-	ORN	1841	2002	*quintessence*	1	RES	1584	1977
arsenicate	-		1757	1951	*quintessentiate*	-		1606	1908
opinion	-	PERF	1555	2002					
opinionate	1		1599	2000					

2.3 Conversion vs *-en* suffixation

Lemma	**S**	**Semantic category**	**Timeline**		**Lemma**	**S**	**Semantic category**	**Timeline**	
			*	†				*	†
black	1	INCH	1225	1500/ 1866	*white1*	2a	CAUS	OE	1724
blacken	1		1300	2003	*whiten*	2c		1552	1997
earth	1a	INST	1450	1995	*white1*	2b	CAUS	OE	1988
earthen	1		1708	1871	*whiten*	2a		1425	2008
hard	1	INCH	eOE	1450	*black*	2a	CAUS	1350	2008
harden	1b		1350	2013	*blacken*	2a		1425	2007
hard	2	CAUS	eOE	1642/ 1844	*black*	2b	CAUS	1568	2009
harden	1a		1200	2014	*blacken*	2c		1730	2002
hard	4	CAUS	OE	1614	*black*	2c	ORN	1579	1999
harden	4a		1350	2005	*blacken*	2b		1699	2008
hard	5	CAUS	500	1618	*black*	2e	CAUS	1811	2009
harden	5		1425	2011	*blacken*	2d		1808	2005
heart	1a	ORN	eOE/ 1830	1681/ 1905	*black*	3a	CAUS	1425	2000
hearten	1		1524	2009	*blacken*	3		1649	1993
heart	3	RES	1573	1573	*mad*	2	CAUS	1425	1924
hearten	2b		1594	2005	*madden*	2		1720	1987
just	-	CAUS	1558	1914	*pink*	1b	INCH	1854	1995
justen	-		1659	1683	*pinken*	1		1890	1991
less	1	INCH	1225	1602	*pink*	2	CAUS	1819	2000
lessen	1		1400	2008	*pinken*	2		1918	1995
less	2a	CAUS	1225/ 1937	1678/ 2003	*plump3*	1a	CAUS	1533	1999
lessen	2a		1410	2009	*plumpen*	1		1687/ 1853	1998
like2	1a	CAUS	1450	2014	*plump3*	2	INCH	1602	1994
liken	2a		1340	2003	*plumpen*	2		1795/ 1966	1999
mist	2a	ORN	1439	1994	*rough2*	1b	CAUS	1728	1996
misten	-		1599	1599	*roughen*	1a		1582	2000

Lemma	S	Semantic category	Timeline		Lemma	S	Semantic category	Timeline	
			*	†				*	†
old	-	INCH	eOE	1741/1999	*rough2*	5	INCH	1876	2008
olden	1		1700	1994	*roughen*	2a		1728	2008
piece	2a	RES	1475	1992	*soft*	6	CAUS	1425	1994
piecen	-		1835	1995	*soften*	4a		1425	2011
*red*1	1	STAT	OE/ 1870	1500/ 1997	*strength*	1a	ORN	1200	1993
redden	2		1648	2004	*strenghthen*	2a		1534	2004
*red*1	1	INCH	OE/ 1870	1500/ 1997	*strength*	2	ORN	1300	2002
redden	4		1648	2004	*strengthen*	4a		1539	2002
*red*1	2	CAUS	1225	1981	*strength*	3	ORN	1325	1984
redden	1a		1552	2002	*strengthen*	1		1450	1995
*rich*1	1	CAUS	1350	1955	*strength*	4a	ORN	1340	2008
richen	1		1795	2008	*strengthen*	3b		1546	2007
*ripe*1	1a	INCH	OE	1935	*earth*	3	ORN	1658	2005
ripen	1b		1573	2006	*earthen*	3		1904	1998
*ripe*1	2a	CAUS	1398	1948	*mad*	1a	INCH	1384	1600/ 1873
ripen	1a		1450	2000	*madden*	1		1704	1913
rooten	-	ORN	1652	1652	*meek*	1b	CAUS	1200	1570
*root*1	7b		1450	1998	*meeken*	1b		1450	1574
rough2	1c	CAUS	1792	1996	*meek*	2	INCH	1400	1540
roughen	4		1864	2008	*meeken*	2		1500/ 1844	1861
sad	1a	CAUS	1384	1924	*big2*	1	CAUS	1884	1890
sadden	1b		1600	1995	*biggen*	1		1643	1955
sad	3a	CAUS	1578	2000	*less*	3	CAUS	1382	1528
sadden	2a		1565	2002	*lessen*	4		1579	2008
smart2	1a	CAUS	1780	1983	*malt*	2	INCH	1733	1873
smarten	2a		1899	2005	*malten*	-		1776	1825
smart2	1b	INCH	1794	1906	*meek*	1a	CAUS	1200	1680
smarten	2c		1813	2001	*meeken*	1a		1400	1880

Lemma	S	Semantic category	Timeline *	Timeline †	Lemma	S	Semantic category	Timeline *	Timeline †
smart2	3a	INCH	1888	2009	*night*	1	INCH	1393	1572
smarten	1b		1899	2005	*nighten*	-		1561	1570
smart2	3b	CAUS	1926	2004	*ripe1*	3	CAUS	1398	1614
smarten	1a		1782	2006	*ripen*	5a		1590	1995
soft	2	CAUS	1225	1669/ 1997	*affrigthten*	-	CAUS	1615	1914
soften	3a		1415	2006	*affright*	1		OE	1995
soft	4	INCH	1300/ 1917	1650/ 1997	*great*	2	CAUS	1440	1656
soften	7a		1565	2005	*greaten*	3a		1613	2008
stark	1a	INCH	OE	1615/ 1996	*hard*	3	CAUS	OE	1543
starken	2		1513	1996	*harden*	3		1200	1917
stark	2	CAUS	1400	1562	*nigh*	1c	LOC	1387	1908
starken	1b		1536	2014	*nighen*	-		1400	1400
trust	1	INST	1225	2002	*mild*	2	CAUS	1340	1628
trusten	-		1382	1908	*milden*	1		1603	1900
quiet	-	INCH	1572	2003	*white1*	1	INCH	eOE	1615
quieten	2		1890	2003	*whiten*	3a		1597	2006

2.4 Conversion vs *-ify* suffixation

Lemma	S	Semantic category	Timeline *	Timeline †	Lemma	S	Semantic category	Timeline *	Timeline †
beautify	1	CAUS	1425	2005	*mummify*	1	INCH	1628	1996
beauty	-		1495	1990	*mummify*	2		1863	1984
happy	-	CAUS	1600	1999	*mummify*	3		1888	1994
happify	-		1612	1995	*mummy*	-		1620/ 1842	1999
jazz	2a	SIM	1915	2000	*prettify*	-	CAUS	1661	2003
jazzify	-		1927	2007	*pretty*	2		1868	1993

Lemma	S	Semantic category	Timeline		Lemma	S	Semantic category	Timeline	
			*	†				*	†
monsterfy	-	RES	1584/ 1996	2001	*prose*	1a	RES	1450	1992
monster	1		1608	1979	*prosify*	1		1774	2004
soul	2	ORN	OE	1966	*verb*	2	RES	1928	2010
soulify	-		1662	1962	*verbify*	-		1820	2004
spruce	1	CAUS	1594	2014	*filthify*	-	CAUS	1624	2003
sprucify	-		1611	2014	*filthy*	-		1581/ 1835	1627/ 2011
lady	2a	RES	1607/ 1989	1616/ 1999	*pulp*	1a	RES	1649	2005
ladyfy	-		1602/ 1859	1682/ 2002	*pulpify*	-		1839	2003
palsify	-	ORN	1882	1882	*truth*	3	SIM	1604	1910
palsy	2		1615	2003	*truthify*	1		1647	1690
terror	1	ORN	1655	1976	*nettle*	1a	ORN	1425	1908
terrify	1		1536	2005	*nettlefy*	-		1602	1602
nullify	2a	CAUS	1607	1987	*nonsense*	1	RES	1681	2002
null1	1a		1556	1987	*nonsensify*	-		1649	1947
statufy	1	ORN	1838	2004	*princify*	-	RES	1847	1847
statue2	1		1611	1989	*prince*	2		1656/ 1873	2005
dunce	2b	RES	1649	2002	*prose*	1b	RES	1788	1834
duncify	-		1594	1989	*prosify*	2		1816	1969
baby	1a	SIM	1744	2003	*nonsense*	1	RES	1681	2002
babyfy	-		1631	2007	*nonsensify*	-		1649	1947
muddify	1	CAUS	1789	1991					
muddy	1a		1604	1992					

2.5 Conversion vs *-ize* suffixation

Lemma	S	Semantic category	Timeline		Lemma	S	Semantic category	Timeline	
			*	†				*	†
action	1	RES	1734	1996	*pattern*	7	RES	1862	2001
actionize	2		1871	1871	*patternize*	2		1836	1991
alphabet	-	INST	1671	1954	*pellet*	1	RES	1609/ 1936	1990
alphabetize	1		1691	2005	*pelletize*	-		1952	1992
anthem	-	RES	1628	1997	*pilgrim*	-	SIM	1561	2002
anthemize	-		1827	2008	*pilgrimize*	1		1609	1976
autograph	2	RES	1833	2006	*politic*	1	INCH	1892	1992
autographize	-		1822	1906	*politicize*	1		1758	1991
biographize	-	RES	1793	2002	*posture*	3a	PERF	1790	2001
biography	-		1794	2002	*posturize*	2		1850	1993
character	4	PERF	1618	2008	*powder1*	8a	RES	1400	1991
characterize	4		1610	2010	*powderize*	2		1903	1998
civil	-	CAUS	1584	1591	*powder1*	9	RES	1526	1993
civilize	1a		1595	2000	*powderize*	2		1954	1954
companion	1	ORN	1616/ 1831	2009	*powder1*	9	INCH	1526	1993
companionize	1		1787	1926	*powderize*	2		1954	1954
companion	2	STAT	1622	2011	*prologue*	1	SIM	1616	2002
companionize	2		1870	1994	*prologuize*	-		1749	2000
dialogue	1a	PERF	1595	2006	*pulpit*	2	INST	1540/ 1923	1643/ 1995
dialoguize	-		1596	2000	*pulpitize*	1		1649/ 1875	2006
feminine	-	CAUS	1583	1949	*pulpit*	2	INST	1540/ 1923	1643/ 1995
femininize	2		1864	2003	*pulpitize*	2		1798	2002
funeral	1	PERF	1578/ 1840	2001	*rhapsodize*	4b	PERF	1819	2002
funeralize	2b		1863	2012	*rhapsody*	2a		1847	2002

Lemma	S	Semantic category	Timeline		Lemma	S	Semantic category	Timeline	
			*	†				*	†
hazard	5	RES	1569	2014	*rhapsodize*	4a	PERF	1787	1994
hazardize	-		1616/ 1865	1657/ 1997	*rhapsody*	2b		1847	1999
heaven	-	CAUS	1614/ 1839	1650/ 1970	*rhythm*	2b	ORN	1889	2008
heavenize	-		1651/ 1844	1680/ 1940	*rhythmize*	2		1862	1994
humor	1b	STAT	1598	1982	*ridicule*	1	ORN	1680	2006
humorize	1		1598	1598	*ridiculize*	-		1615	2001
marble	2a	ORN	1675	1990	*rubber*	1	ORN	1892	1998
marbleize	-		1854	1989	*rubberize2*	-		1903	2004
method	-	INST	1607	1640	*satin*	-	ORN	1839	1998
methodize	1		1586	1989	*satinize*	-		1865	2008
mirror	3a	INST	1827	1992	*satire*	-	PERF	1602	2003
mirrorize	-		1598	1873	*satirize*	2a		1619	2009
mission	2a	PERF	1772	1894	*signal*	1b	STAT	1866	2006
missionize	2		1875	2005	*signalize*	5		1808	2008
model	3	INST	1605	1990	*sonnet*	3	RES	1598	2010
modelize	1		1600	1995	*sonnetize*	2		1799	1994
pander	2	SIM	1641	1996	*aerosol*	1	RES	1964	1998
panderize	-		1598	1638	*aerosolize*	1		1944	2001
parrot	1	SIM	1596	2002	*canal*	1b	RES	1799	2012
parrotize	1		1647	1789	*canalize*	1a		1830	2015
particular	-	CAUS	1605	1646/ 1979	*legend*	1a	RES	1597	1942
particularize	2a		1593	1987	*legendize*	-		1859	2002
patternize	1	INST	1615	1615	*legend*	3	ORN	1886	2007
pattern	1a		1567	2001	*legendize*	1		1859	2002
peacock	2	SIM	1654/ 1818	1990	*proselyte*	1b	CAUS	1800	1996
peacockize	-		1598	1598	*proselytize*	1		1679	2001
photograph	1a	PERF	1839	2004	*proselyte*	1a	RES	1624	2001
photographize	-		1841	1974	*proselytize*	2		1796	1994

Lemma	S	Semantic category	Timeline *	Timeline †	Lemma	S	Semantic category	Timeline *	Timeline †
powder1	4a	ORN	1616	2002	*revolution*	-	ORN	1805	1997
powderize	1		1800	1800	*revolutionize*	1		1795	2005
pressure	1	ORN	1945	2002	*woman*	1a	CAUS	1586	2004
pressurize	2		1911	2003	*womanize*	1a		1611	2007
pressure	2	ORN	1961	2000	*channel*	2a	INST	1560	2008
pressurize	1		1940	2002	*channelize*	-		1609/ 1860	2015
procession	3a	PERF	1706	1997	*medal*	1	ORN	1860	2007
processionize	-		1774	1906	*medallize*	3		1858	2014
psalmodize	1	PERF	1513/ 1850	2002	*monologue*	1	PERF	1825	1986
psalmody	1		1475	1492	*monologuize*	-		1870	1998
raven	1b	PERF	1570	2006	*pillorize*	-	ORN	1647	2002
ravenize	-		1677	1677	*pillory*	2		1699	2001
requisition	1a	PERF	1800	2000	*factor*	3	RES	1859	2010
requisitionize	-		1834	1995	*factorize*	2a		1877	2011
rhapsodize	2b	PERF	1846	1964	*adjective*	1	RES	1802	2004
rhapsody	1		1699	1822	*adjectivize*	-		1848	1949
romantic	-	CAUS	1926	1972	*melodize*	1	PERF	1662	2002
romanticize	1		1818	2007	*melody*	1		1595/ 1841	1989
signal	2b	RES	1845	1998	*acronym*	-	RES	1967	2005
signalize	4c		1838	1906	*acronymize*	-		1955	2004
signal	2b	INST	1845	1998	*emotion*	2	ORN	1875	2008
signalize	4c		1838	1906	*emotionize*	-		1855	2008
station	all	ORN	1609	2009	*satellite*	1	SIM	1596	2009
stationize	-		1598	1598	*satellitize*	2		1887	1990
summer1	1a	PERF	1440	2000	*emperize*	-	SIM	1601	1631
summerize	1		1797	1941	*empery*	-		1503	1503
verbal	1b	INST	1974	1996	*epicure*	-	SIM	1628	1655
verbalize	1		1609	2008	*epicurize*	3		1707	1835

Lemma	S	Semantic category	Timeline *	Timeline †	Lemma	S	Semantic category	Timeline *	Timeline †
mongrel	-	RES	1602	1662/ 1941	*paragon*	3	STAT	1617	1623
mongrelize	1		1629	1991	*paragonize*	2		1592	1592
oval	1	CAUS	1665	1990	*paragon*	4	STAT	1620	1872
ovalize	-		1909	2000	*paragonize*	3		1606	1635
parallel	3	CAUS	1646	1969	*period*	-	CAUS	1595	1755
parallelize	4a		1853	1993	*periodize*	1		1657	1683
savage	2	CAUS	1611	1910	*ruffian*	2b	SIM	1817	1899
savagize	-		1794	2005	*ruffianize*	2		1817	1888
union	-	PERF	1475	2006	*melancholize*	1	RES	1598	1668
unionize	2a		1872	2004	*melancholy*	1		1492	1980
wanton	2	CAUS	1582	1998	*sonnet*	2	RES	1593	1878
wantonize	2		1606	2010	*sonnetize*	1		1798	1829
wanton	4a	SIM	1634	2011	*bumper1*	1	SIM	1691	1879
wantonize	1c		1673	1673	*bumperize*	-		1794	1964
alkali	1	ORN	1849	1849	*character*	2	ORN	1555	1831
alkalize	-		1666	2000	*characterize*	2		1594	2004
artery	-		1843	2006	*husband*	5		1545	2001
arterize	-	ORN	1600	1600	*husbandize*	-	SIM	1625	1649/ 1969
atom	-	RES	1648	1779	*microscope*	-	INST	1888	1991
atomize	1a		1645	2007	*microscopize*	-		1846	1846
scenario	-	RES	1923	1974	*missionarize*	2	SIM	1853	1987
scenarize	-		1915	1992	*missionary*	2		1884	1983
philosophize	1a	SIM	1594	1999	*niggard*	1	SIM	1596	1625
philosophy	-		1382	2002	*niggardize*	-		1606	1654
propaganda	-	INST	1921	2005	*oracle*	1	SIM	1595	1952
propagandize	1		1844	1994	*oraclize*	1		1648	1648
adjective	2	INST	1804	1990	*oracle*	2	SIM	1654	1866
adjectivize	-		1898	2008	*oraclize*	2		1709	1709
alchemize	2		1658	2009	*paragon*	1		1586	1903
alchemy	-	INST	1615/ 1911	1628/ 2010	*paragonize*	1	INST	1589	1656

Lemma	S	Semantic category	Timeline		Lemma	S	Semantic category	Timeline	
			*	†				*	†
blackguard	2	SIM	1786	2003	*parodize*	1	RES	1657	1681/ 1994
blackguardize	-		1777	1966	*parody*	1b		1781	1991
character	5a	ORN	1621	2006	*ruffian*	1a	SIM	1594/ 1869	1601/ 1901
characterize	5		1786	2009	*ruffianize*	1a		1611/ 1867	1894
character	5b	STAT	1621	2006	*canal*	1a	ORN	1792	2010
characterize	3		1602	2010	*canalize*	1b		1860	2014
emphase	-	ORN	1631/ 1849	1947	*paroxytone*	-	CAUS	1890	1890
emphasize	2		1793	2010	*paroxytonize*	-		1904	1930
miniature	1	CAUS	1686	2000	*pemmican*	-	CAUS	1837	1839
miniaturize	-		1909	2000	*pemmicanize*	-		1845	1935
orphan	-	RES	1814	2002	*wanton*	1f	SIM	1628	1990
orphanize	-		1797	1989	*wantonize*	1a		1592	1826
pallet2	-	INST	1989	2002	*woman*	1b	SIM	1613	1911
palletize	-		1953	2003	*womanize*	1b		1604	1869
parasite	2	SIM	1882	1998	*woman*	1b	INCH	1613	1911
parasitize	1		1872	1997	*womanize*	1b		1604	1869
parodize	2	INST	1768	1998	*character*	1	INST	1555	1963
parody	2		1801	2002	*characterize*	1		1581	1886
parrot	2	SIM	1640	2002	*morsel*	1	RES	1598	1920
parrotize	2		1997	1997	*morselize*	-		1894	1994

2.6 *-ate* vs *-ize*

Lemma	S	Semantic category	Timeline		Lemma	S	Semantic category	Timeline	
			*	†				*	†
aluminate	-	ORN	1934	2003	*platinate*	-	ORN	1858	1897
aluminize2	-		1888	2003	*platinize*	-		1825	1986
objectivate	-	CAUS	1860	2001	*probabilize*	-	CAUS	1804	2002
objectivize	-		1825	1985	*probablize*	-		1847	2005
oxygenate	1	ORN	1789	1994	*religionate*	-	ORN	1676	1676
oxygenize	-		1802	1993	*religionize*	2		1783	2000
fluoridize	1	ORN	1940	2008	*rhetoricate*	1	INST	1617	1880
fluoridate	1		1949	1996	*rhetoricize*	1		1676	2007
nitrogenate	-	ORN	1927	1995	*rhetoricate*	2	CAUS	1662/ 1841	1924
nitrogenize	-		1871	1978	*rhetoricize*	2		1855	1994
maximate	-	RES	1881	1993	*oxidize*	2	RES	1823	1993
maximize	1		1817	1995	*oxidate*	2		1789	1879
memorate	2	INST	1983	1983	*peroxidate*	-	RES	1822	1986
memorize	3		1834	1978	*peroxidize*	1		1821	2002
metricate	2	CAUS	1965	1972	*carbonate2*	-	ORN	1922	2000
metricize2	-		1906	1965	*carbonize*	3		1888	2000
nebulate	1	INCH	1753	1753	*minorate*	-	CAUS	1534	1682/ 1920
nebulize	2		1891	1891	*minorize*	1		1615	1641
pedestrianate	a	SIM	1845	1998	*myelinate*	1	ORN	1890	1995
pedestrianize	1		1811	1995	*myelinize*	-		1903	1903
pendulate	1	SIM	1698	1987	*phosphorate*	-	ORN	1836	2004
pendulize	-		1869	1869	*phosphorize*	2		1927	1927

2.7 *-ify* vs *-ize*

Lemma	S	Semantic category	Timeline *	Timeline †	Lemma	S	Semantic category	Timeline *	Timeline †
acetify	2	INCH	1854	1985	*objectify*	1	RES	1854	1989
acetize	-		1859	1859	*objectize*	-		1817	2001
alkalify	1	RES	1790	2007	*devilify*	-	RES	1645	2007
alkalize	-		1666	2000	*devilize*	2		1656	2006
Anglicify	-	CAUS	1859	1889	*probabilize*	-	CAUS	1804	2002
anglicize	1		1710	2000	*probablize*	-		1847	2005
etherify	-	RES	1800	2006	*plasticize*	2	ORN	1940	1993
etherize	2a		1803	2010	*plastify*	2		1972	2004
humanify	-	RES	1630	1999	*rigidify*	1	INCH	1829	1999
humanize	-		1603	2000	*rigidize*	1		1858	2007
iconify	-	RES	1986	2003	*rigidify*	2	CAUS	1842	2002
iconize	-		1986	2002	*rigidize*	2		1936	2006
magnetify	1	RES	1649	1649	*oxidize*	2	RES	1823	1993
magnetize	3a		1792	1988	*oxidate*	2		1789	1879
magnetify	2	RES	1785	1797	*resinify*	1	RES	1804	2006
magnetize	2		1784	1991	*resinize*	-		1848	1912
artify	-	CAUS	1662	1996	*substantify*	-	ORN	1605/ 1846	2008
artize	2		1603	1603	*substantize*	2		1610	1993
electrize	-	ORN	1747	1967	*churchify*	-	ORN	1719	2003
electrify	1a		1745	2000	*churchize*	-		1843	2001
hotelize	-	RES	1886	2007	*acidify*	1a	ORN	1783	1990
hotelify	-		1834	2007	*acidize*	-		1852	2007
nullize	-	CAUS	1615	1615	*virtuefy*	-	CAUS	1768	2005
nullify	3		1609	1988	*virtuize*	1		1828	2008
Germanify	-	CAUS	1863	2006	*ozonify*	-	RES	1859	1866
Germanize	2		1608	2002	*ozonize*	2		1866	1893
					pyritify	-	ORN	1800	1829
					pyritize	-		1860	1997

Appendix 3: Corpus data for triplets

	EHCB		COHA		COCA		iWeb
	raw	per mil	raw	per mil	raw	per mil	
Anglicize	1	>0.01	-	-	49	0.05	101
Anglify	1	>0.01	-	-	-	-	-
Anglize	-	-	-	-	-	-	-
carbonate	2	>0.01	17	0.04	-	-	3705
carbonify	-	-	-	-	-	-	-
carbonize	-	-	23	0.06	24	0.02	142
empatron	-	-	-	-	-	-	-
patron	-	-	-	-	-	-	-
patronise	119	0.12	86	0.21	-	-	559
patronize	1700	1.72	1355	3.35	1389	1.4	7078
Englify	-	-	-	-	-	-	-
English	1592	1.61	-	-	145	0.15	4677
Englishify	-	-	-	-	-	-	-
Englishize	-	-	-	-	-	-	-
enthrone	527	0.53	48	0.12	248	0.25	196
enthronize	10	0.01	-	-	-	-	-
throne	422	0.43	-	-	-	-	-
thronize	-	-	-	-	-	-	-
thrononize	-	-	-	-	-	-	-
fossil	-	-	-	-	-	-	-
fossilate	-	-	-	-	-	-	-
fossilify	-	-	-	-	-	-	-
fossilize	-	-	51	0.13	190	0.19	1637
French	-	-	-	-	9	0.01	-
Frenchify	112	0.11	-	-	-	-	-
Frenchize	-	-	-	-	-	-	-
function	163	0.17	4002	9.88	20370	20.51	360237
functionate	-	-	-	-	-	-	-
functionize	-	-	-	-	-	-	-

	EHCB		COHA		COCA		iWeb
	raw	**per mil**	**raw**	**per mil**	**raw**	**per mil**	
gangrenate	3	>0.01	-	-	-	-	-
gangrene	126	0.13	4	0.01	3	0	-
gangrenize	-	-	-	-	-	-	-
god	-	-	-	-	-	-	-
godify	-	-	-	-	-	-	-
godize	-	-	-	-	-	-	-
historify	2	>0.01	-	-	-	-	-
historize	7	0.01	-	-	-	-	-
history	-	-	-	-	-	-	-
immune	-	-	-	-	-	-	-
immunify	-	-	-	-	-	-	-
immunize	-	-	207	0.51	818	0.82	8044
metre	-	-	-	-	-	-	-
metrify	4	>0.01	-	-	-	-	-
metrize	-	-	-	-	-	-	-
mission	2	>0.01	-	-	-	-	-
missionate	-	-	-	-	-	-	-
missionize	-	-	1	0	10	0.01	22
moist	88	0.09	-	-	-	-	-
moisten	1200	1.22	1274	3.12	1043	1.05	13650
moistify	-	-	-	-	-	-	-
neat	-	-	-	-	-	-	-
neaten	-	-	24	0.06	57	0.06	1205
neatify	-	-	-	-	-	-	-
parcel	528	0.53	297	0.73	315	0.32	1157
parcellate	-	-	-	-	-	-	-
parcellize	-	-	-	-	-	-	-
pasivate	-	-	-	-	2	0	-
passivify	-	-	-	-	-	-	-
passivize	-	-	-	-	-	-	-

	EHCB		COHA		COCA		iWeb
	raw	**per mil**	**raw**	**per mil**	**raw**	**per mil**	
patinate	-	-	2	0	8	0.01	-
patine	-	-	-	-	-	-	-
patinize	-	-	-	-	-	-	-
pauper	-	-	-	-	-	-	-
pauperate	-	-	-	-	-	-	-
pauperize	-	-	32	0.08	6	0.01	-
perfection	-	-	-	-	-	-	-
perfectionate	34	0.03	-	-	-	-	-
perfectionize	-	-	-	-	-	-	-
personate	1731	1.75	96	0.24	-	-	-
personify	39	0.04	709	1.75	1480	1.49	13885
personize	3	>0.01	-	-	-	-	-
quiet	7455	7.54	2612	6.45	2355	2.37	12964
quieten	-	-	50	0.12	68	0.07	2028
quietize	-	-	-	-	-	-	-
resin	56	0.06	-	-	-	-	-
resinate	-	-	-	-	-	-	-
resinize	-	-	-	-	-	-	-
statue2	5	>0.01	-	-	-	-	-
statuefy	-	-	-	-	-	-	-
statuize	-	-	-	-	-	-	-
storify	-	-	-	-	-	-	-
storize	1	>0.01	-	-	-	-	-
story	321	0.33	2	0	1	0	-

Appendix 4: Corpus data for doublets

	EHCB		COHA		COCA		iWeb
	raw	per mil	raw	per mil	raw	per mil	
acetify	-	-	-	-	-	-	-
acetize	-	-	-	-	-	-	-
acidify	2.00	>0.01	22	0.05	134	0.13	2793
acidize	-	-	-	-	-	-	-
acronym	-	-	-	-	1	0	-
acronymize	-	-	-	-	-	-	-
action	-	-	208	0.51	-	-	20865
actionize	-	-	-	-	-	-	-
activate	4	>0.01	977	2.41	11311	11.39	422032
active	-	-	-	-	-	-	-
adjective	-	-	-	-	-	-	-
adjectivize	-	-	-	-	3	0	-
aerosol	-	-	-	-	-	-	-
aerosolize	-	-	-	-	10	0.01	88
alchemize	-	-	3	0.01	5	0.01	-
alchemy	-	-	-	-	-	-	-
alembic	-	-	-	-	-	-	-
alembicate	-	-	-	-	-	-	-
alkali	-	-	-	-	-	-	-
alkalify	1	>0.01	-	-	-	-	-
alkalize	4	>0.01	-	-	-	-	-
alphabet	-	-	-	-	-	-	-
alphabetize	-	1	>0.01	21	0.05	169	0.17
aluminate	-	-	-	-	-	-	-
aluminize	-	-	1	0	1	0	-
Anglicify	-	-	-	-	-	-	-
anglicize	1	>0.01	21	0.05	49	0.05	101
anthem	-	-	-	-	-	-	-
anthemize	-	-	-	-	-	-	-

	EHCB		COHA		COCA		iWeb
	raw	per mil	raw	per mil	raw	per mil	
arsenic	-	-	-	-	-	-	-
arsenicate	-	-	-	-	-	-	-
arterize	-	-	-	-	-	-	-
artery	-	-	-	-	-	-	-
artify	-	-	-	-	2	0	-
artize	2	>0.01	-	-	-	-	-
atom	-	-	-	-	-	-	-
atomize	4	>0.01	46	0.11	228	0.23	1753
autograph	-	-	263	0.65	862	0.87	10639
autographize	-	-	-	-	-	-	-
baby	9	0.01	88	0.22	179	0.18	1731
babyfy	-	-	-	-	-	-	-
beautify	5049	5.11	616	1.52	411	0.41	11364
beauty	-	-	1	0	-	-	-
belimb	-	-	-	-	-	-	-
limb	242	0.25	24	0.06	18	0.02	45
belittle	9	0.01	665	1.64	1932	1.95	13667
little	-	-	-	-	-	-	-
belord	-	-	-	-	-	-	-
lord	4481	4.54	206	0.51	254	0.26	2430
biograph	-	-	2	0	7	0.01	-
biographize	-	-	-	-	-	-	-
biography	-	-	-	-	-	-	-
black	395	0.4	855	2.11	1924	1.94	14907
blacken	1091	1.11	1371	3.39	1151	1.16	8259
blackguard	10	0.01	-	-	-	-	-
blackguardize	-	-	-	-	-	-	-
bumper	40	0.04	-	-	-	-	-
bumperize	-	-	-	-	-	-	-
canal	8	0.01	-	-	-	-	-
canalise	-	-	3	0.01	1	0	-
canalize	-	-	41	0.1	12	0.01	-

	EHCB		COHA		COCA		iWeb
	raw	per mil	raw	per mil	raw	per mil	
carbonate	2	>0.01	17	0.04	-	-	3705
carbonize	-	-	23	0.06	24	0.02	142
channel	126	0.13	799	1.97	5585	5.62	82547
channelize	-	-	2	0	16	0.02	-
character	442	0.45	9	0.02	2	0	-
characterise	224	0.23	-	-	-	-	-
characterize	1244	1.26	7537	18.61	22667	22.82	219122
churchify	-	-	-	-	-	-	-
churchize	-	-	-	-	-	-	-
civil	-	-	-	-	-	-	-
civilise	9	0.01	-	-	-	-	168
civilize	775	0.79	-	-	-	-	1379
companion	279	0.28	23	0.06	7	0.01	-
companionize	-	-	-	-	-	-	-
culturate	-	-	-	-	-	-	-
culture	53	0.05	106	0.26	672	0.68	6029
devilify	-	-	-	-	-	-	-
devilize	1	>0.01	-	-	-	-	-
dialogise	1	>0.01	-	-	-	-	-
dialogize	9	0.01	-	-	2	0	-
dialogue	44	0.04	-	-	-	-	-
dialoguize	-	-	-	-	-	-	-
dunce	-	-	-	-	-	-	-
duncify	-	-	-	-	-	-	-
earth	1977	2	29	0.07	37	0.04	740
earthen	-	-	-	-	-	-	-
electrify	285	0.29	668	1.65	1176	1.18	12372
electrize	2	>0.01	-	-	-	-	-
emotion	-	-	-	-	-	-	-
emotionize	-	-	-	-	-	-	-
empacket	-	-	-	-	-	-	-
packet	14	0.01	13	0.03	47	0.05	2000

	EHCB		COHA		COCA		iWeb
	raw	per mil	raw	per mil	raw	per mil	
empanel	146	0.15	43	0.11	75	0.08	217
panel	10	0.01	36	0.09	251	0.25	256
empeople	-	-	-	-	-	-	-
people	4901	4.96	1469	3.63	465	0.47	3408
emperize	1	>0.01	-	-	-	-	-
empery	-	-	-	-	-	-	-
emphase	-	-	-	-	-	-	-
emphasize	1	>0.01	9587	23.67	34190	34.43	342506
emplaster	1	>0.01	-	-	-	-	-
plaster	106	0.11	1344	3.32	2259	2.27	17815
emplume	1	>0.01	-	-	-	-	-
plume	850	0.86	243	0.6	-	-	233
empoison	64	0.06	-	-	-	-	-
poison	2831	2.87	3195	7.89	7206	7.26	59906
empowder	-	-	-	-	-	-	-
powder	2983	3.02	936	2.31	835	0.84	12927
empower	1473	1.49	1693	4.18	9398	9.46	209170
power	1889	1.91	1182	2.92	8947	9.01	305781
empurple	3	>0.01	-	-	-	-	-
purple	-	-	141	0.35	39	0.04	116
enjewel	-	-	-	-	-	-	-
jewel	79	0.08	84	0.21	8	0.01	238
enqueue	-	-	-	-	4	0	-
queue	17	0.02	162	0.4	1015	1.02	4354
enrich	12437	12.6	3079	7.6	6275	6.32	103308
rich	3	>0.01	-		-	-	-
epicure	-	-	4	0.01	2	0	-
epicurise	1	>0.01	-	-	-	-	-
epicurize	4	>0.01	-	-	-	-	-
etherify	-	-	-	-	-	-	-
etherize	-	-	-	-	2	0	-

	EHCB		COHA		COCA		iWeb
	raw	per mil	raw	per mil	raw	per mil	
faction	-	-	-	-	-	-	-
factionate	-	-	-	-	-	-	-
factor	7	0.01	127	0.31	2710	2.73	59655
factorize	-	-	3	0.01	5	0.01	-
femine	-	-	3	0.01	1	0	-
feminine	-	-	-	-	-	-	-
femininize	-	-	-	-	-	-	-
feminise	-	-	-	-	4	0	-
feminize	3	>0.01	39	0.1	226	0.23	2114
filthify	-	-	-	-	-	-	-
filthy	-	-	-	-	-	-	-
fluoridate	-	-	5	0.01	27	0.03	-
fluoridize	-	-	-	-	-	-	-
funeral	-	-	-	-	-	-	-
funeralize	-	-	2	0	2	0	-
Germanify	-	-	-	-	-	-	-
Germanize	6	0.01	5	0.01	3	0	-
happify	14	0.01	-	-	-	-	-
happy	-	-	-	-	-	-	-
hard	-	-	-	-	-	-	-
harden	19687	10.83	3288	8.12	4937	4.97	82553
hazard	9946	10.07	1206	2.98	586	0.59	6331
hazardize	1	>0.01	-	-	-	-	-
heart	6504	6.59	-	-	-	-	-
hearten	563	0.57	362	0.89	657	0.66	3818
heaven	-	-	-	-	-	-	-
hevanize	-	-	-	-	-	-	-
hotelify	-	-	-	-	-	-	-
hotelize	-	-	-	-	-	-	-
humanify	-	-	-	-	-	-	-
humanize	223	0.23	324	0.8	987	0.99	7575

	EHCB		COHA		COCA		iWeb
	raw	per mil	raw	per mil	raw	per mil	
humor	-	-	698	1.72	-	-	4962
humour	-	-	36	0.09	-	-	-
humourize	-	-	-	-	-	-	-
husband	1906	1.93	261	0.64	335	0.34	1089
husbandize	1	>0.01	-	-	-	-	-
iconify	-	-	-	-	-	-	-
iconize	-	-	-	-	-	-	-
jazz	-	-	13	0.03	51	0.05	1394
jazzify	-	-	-	-	-	-	-
just	4797	4.86	-	-	-	-	-
justen	5	0.01	-	-	5	0.01	-
lady	-	-	2	0	-	-	-
ladyfy	3	>0.01	-	-	-	-	-
legend	-	-	-	-	-	-	-
legendize	-	-	-	-	-	-	-
less	-	-	-	-	-	-	-
lessen	9660	9.78	4391	10.84	4936	4.97	79102
like	85178	86.28	160827	397.1	614689	619.01	6685482
liken	3057	3.1	1190	2.94	3500	3.52	32486
mad	1306	1.32	-	-	-	-	-
madden	94	0.1	2221	5.48	2941	2.96	32127
magnetify	-	-	-	-	-	-	-
magnetize	6	0.01	152	0.38	195	0.2	3763
marble	145	0.15	-	-	-	0	-
marbleize	-	-	-	-	5	0.01	37
margin	87	0.09	-	-	-	-	-
marginate	4	>0.02	-	-	-	-	-
maximate	-	-	-	-	-	-	-
maximize	-	-	660	1.63	9899	9.97	348100
medal	18	0.02	-	-	-	-	-
medallize	-	-	-	-	-	-	-
melancholize	6	0.01	-	-	-	-	-
melancholy	-	-	-	-	-	-	-

	EHCB		COHA		COCA		iWeb
	raw	per mil	raw	per mil	raw	per mil	
melodise	2	0.01	-	-	-	-	-
melodize	12	0.01	-	-	-	-	-
melody	-	-	-	-	-	-	-
memorate	4	>0.01	-	-	-	-	-
memorise	22	0.02	-	-	-	-	-
memorize	193	0.2	1387	3.42	4914	4.95	61111
method	-	-	2	0	-	-	-
methodize	346	0.35	0	0	-	-	-
metricate	-	-	-	-	-	-	-
metricize	-	-	-	-	-	-	-
microscope	-	-	-	-	-	-	-
microscopize	-	-	-	-	-	-	-
miniature	-	-	-	-	-	-	-
miniaturize	-	-	1	0	2	0.23	1994
mirror	128	0.13	1159	2.86	5009	5.04	77298
mirrorize	-	-	-	-	-	-	-
mission	3	>0.01	-	-	-	-	-
missionarize	-	-	-	-	-	-	-
missionary	-	-	-	-	-	-	-
missionize	-	-	-	-	10	0.01	22
mist	1007	1.02	317	0.78	578	0.58	15788
misten	-	-	-	-	-	-	-
model	-	-	2424	5.99	-	-	2177224
modellize	-	-	-	-	-	-	-
mongrel	-	-	-	-	-	-	-
mongrelize	-	-	1	0	1	0	-
monologize	-	-	-	-	-	-	-
monologue	-	-	-	-	-	-	-
monologuize	-	-	-	-	-	-	-
monster	-	-	-	-	-	-	-
monsterfy	-	-	-	-	-	-	-

	EHCB		COHA		COCA		iWeb
	raw	per mil	raw	per mil	raw	per mil	
morsel	4	>0.01	-	-	-	-	-
moselize	-	-	-	-	-	-	-
motivate	-	-	1556	3.84	19758	19.9	295484
motive	259	0.26	-	-	-	-	-
muddify	-	-	-	-	-	-	-
muddy	230	0.23	173	0.43	488	0.49	3502
mummify	-	-	13	0.03	58	0.06	445
mummy	-	-	-	-	-	-	-
myelinate	-	-	-	-	-	-	-
myelinize	-	-	-	-	-	-	-
nervate	-	-	-	-	-	-	-
nerve	153	0.15	902	2.23	-	-	4992
niggard	1	>0.01	-	-	-	-	-
niggardize	15	0.02	-	-	-	-	-
nitrate	-	-	-	-	-	-	-
nitre	-	-	-	-	-	-	-
nitrogenate	-	-	-	-	-	-	-
nitrogenize	-	-	-	-	-	-	-
null	-	-	9	0.02	31	0.03	49
nullify	522	0.53	943	2.33	1362	1.37	16915
nullify	522	0.53	943	2.33	1362	1.37	16915
nullize	-	-	-	-	-	-	-
objectify	-	-	89	0.22	885	0.89	5376
objectivate	-	-	-	-	-	-	-
objectivize	-	-	1	0	3	0	-
objectize	-	-	-	-	-	-	-
old	-	-	-	-	-	-	-
olden	-	-	-	-	-	-	-
opinion	-	-	-	-	-	-	-
opinionate	21	0.02	6	0.01	4	0	-
orphan	64	0.06	56	0.14	132	0.13	1837
orphanize	-	-	-	-	-	-	-

	EHCB		COHA		COCA		iWeb
	raw	per mil	raw	per mil	raw	per mil	
oval	-	-	-	-	-	-	-
ovalize	-	-	1	0	3	0	-
oxidate	1	>0.01	-	-	-	-	-
oxidize	-	-	352	0.87	595	0.6	20377
oxygenate	28	0.03	23	0.06	152	0.15	3389
oxygenize	-	-	-	-	-	-	-
pallet	-	-	-	-	-	-	-
palletize	-	-	1	0	3	0	-
palsify	-	-	-	-	-	-	-
palsy	-	-	59	0.15	11	0.01	-
pander	-	-	432	1.07	-	-	11675
panderize	-	-	-	-	-	-	-
parallel	1661	1.68	1067	2.63	2978	3	29319
parallelize	5	0.01	-	-	-	-	-
parasite	-	-	-	-	-	-	-
parasitize	-	-	40	0.1	132	0.13	939
parodize	3	>0.01	-	-	-	-	-
parody	29	0.03	252	0.62	1169	1.18	9425
paroxytone	-	-	-	-	-	-	-
paroxytonize	-	-	-	-	-	-	-
parrot	28	0.03	13	0.03	629	0.63	628
parrotize	-	-	-	-	-	-	-
particular	-	-	-	-	-	-	-
particularise	100	0.1	4	0.01	1	0	-
particularize	1215	1.23	150	0.37	105	0.11	514
particulate	-	-	32	0.08	296	0.3	4233
patron	-	-	-	-	-	-	-
patronise	-	-	-	-	52	0.05	559
patronize	-	-	-	-	1389	1.04	7078
pattern	75	0.08	156	0.39	468	0.47	7124
patternize	1	>0.01	-	-	-	-	-

	EHCB		COHA		COCA		iWeb
	raw	per mil	raw	per mil	raw	per mil	
pauper	-	-	-	-	-	-	-
pauperize	-	-	-	-	6	0.01	-
peacock	13	0.01	-	-	-	-	-
peacockise	1	>0.01	-	-	-	-	-
peacockize	-	-	-	-	-	-	-
pellet	23	0.02	-	-	-	-	-
pelletize	-	-	-	-	-	-	-
pemmican	-	-	-	-	-	-	-
pemmicanize	-	-	-	-	-	-	-
pendulate	-	-	-	-	-	-	-
pendulize	-	-	-	-	-	-	-
period	-	-	1	0	-	-	-
periodize	6	0.01	3	0.01	10	0.01	-
peroxidate	-	-	-	-	-	-	-
peroxidize	-	-	-	-	-	-	-
petition	5047	5.11	1199	2.96	2687	2.71	30686
petitionate	1	>0.01	-	-	-	-	-
philosophate	-	-	-	-	-	-	-
philosophize	306	0.31	381	0.94	321	0.32	1810
philosophy	-	-	-	-	-	-	-
phosphorate	-	-	-	-	-	-	-
phosphorize	-	-	-	-	-	-	-
photograph	-	-	5152	12.72	27239	27.43	158464
photographize	-	-	-	-	-	-	-
piece	797	0.81	702	1.73	1982	2	29756
piecen	-	-	-	-	-	-	-
pilgrim	-	-	-	-	-	-	-
pilgrimize	1	>0.01	-	-	-	0	-
pillorize	3	>0.01	-	-	-	-	-
pillory	64	0.06	140	0.35	376	0.38	1835
pink	147	0.15	54	0.13	43	0.04	455
pinken	-	-	5	0.01	5	0.01	-

	EHCB		COHA		COCA		iWeb
	raw	per mil	raw	per mil	raw	per mil	
plasticize	-	-	-	-	-	-	-
plastify	-	-	-	-	2	0	-
platinate	-	-	-	-	-	-	-
platinize	-	-	-	-	-	-	-
plump	148	0.15	518	1.28	646	0.65	10137
plumpen	-	-	-	-	-	-	-
politic	-	-	2	0	-	0	-
politicize	-	-	107	0.26	1	1.97	4909
posture	284	0.29	156	0.39	768	0.77	4367
posturize	-	-	-	-	-	-	-
powder	2983	3.02	936	2.31	835	0.84	12927
powderize	-	-	-	-	-	-	-
pressure	33	0.03	640	1.58	5846	5.89	46169
pressurize	-	-	72	0.18	497	0.5	10508
prettify	2	>0.01	22	0.05	37	0.04	476
pretty	-	-	22	0.05	38	0.04	188
probabilify	-	-	-	-	-	-	-
probabilize	-	-	-	-	-	-	-
probablize	-	-	-	-	-	-	-
procession	40	0.04	1	0	-	-	-
processionize	-	-	-	-	-	-	-
prologize	1	>0.01	-	-	-	-	-
prologue	73	0.07	-	-	-	-	-
prologuize	1	>0.01	-	-	-	-	-
propagand	-	-	-	-	-	-	-
propaganda	-	-	-	-	-	-	-
propagandize	-	-	106	0.26	194	0.2	837
prose	62	0.06	1	0	-	-	-
prosify	1	>0.01	-	-	-	-	-
proselyte	209	0.21	-	-	-	-	-
proselytise	-	-	-	-	11	0.01	-
proselytize	2	>0.01	119	0.29	731	0.74	3074

	EHCB		COHA		COCA		iWeb
	raw	per mil	raw	per mil	raw	per mil	
psalmodize	-	-	-	-	-	-	-
psalmody	-	-	-	-	-	-	-
pulp	45	0.05	114	0.28	211	0.21	2479
pulpify	-	-	-	-	-	-	-
pulpit	-	-	-	-	-	-	-
pulpitize	-	-	-	-	-	-	-
quiet	7445	7.54	2612	6.45	2355	2.37	12964
quieten	-	-	50	0.12	68	0.07	2028
raven	605	0.61	-	-	-	-	-
ravenize	-	-	-	-	-	-	-
red	462	0.47	32	0.08	-	-	1050
redden	374	0.38	1652	4.08	1075	1.08	5471
religionate	-	-	-	-	-	-	-
religionize	-	-	-	-	-	-	-
requisition	1	>0.01	343	0.85	247	0.25	4436
requisitionize	-	-	-	-	-	-	-
resinify	-	-	-	-	-	-	-
resinize	-	-	-	-	-	-	-
revolution	-	-	-	-	-	-	-
revolutionise	-	-	-	-	77	0.08	8307
revolutionize	44	0.04	968	2.39	2654	2.67	45980
rhapsodise	-	-	-	-	2	0	-
rhapsodize	-	-	103	0.25	192	0.19	541
rhapsody	-	-	-	-	-	-	-
rhetoricate	1	>0.01	-	-	-	-	-
rhetoricize	-	-	-	-	-	-	-
rhythm	-	-	-	-	-	-	-
rhythmize	-	-	-	-	-	-	-
rich	3	>0.01	-	-	-	-	-
richen	1	>0.01	-	-	-	-	-
ridicule	2454	2.49	2029	5.01	3687	3.71	25877
ridiculize	2	0.01	-	-	-	-	-

	EHCB		COHA		COCA		iWeb
	raw	per mil	raw	per mil	raw	per mil	
rigidify	-	-	6	0.01	10	0.01	-
rigidize	-	-	-	-	-	-	-
ripe	13	0.01	-	-	-	-	-
ripen	5296	5.36	2508	6.19	1367	1.38	26762
romantic	-	-	-	-	-	-	-
romanticize	-	-	161	0.4	954	0.96	4712
root	13852	14.03	3717	9.18	14773	14.88	156249
rooten	-	-	-	-	1	0	-
rough	174	0.18	897	2.21	1885	1.9	20875
roughen	34	0.03	191	0.47	119	0.12	1798
rubber	3	>0.01	-	-	-	-	-
rubberize	-	-	-	-	-	-	-
sad	199	0.2	-	-	-	-	-
sadden	183	0.19	1122	2.77	3043	3.06	30363
satellite	-	-	-	-	-	-	-
satellize	-	-	-	-	-	-	-
satin	-	-	-	-	-	-	-
satinize	-	-	-	-	-	-	-
satire	13	0.01	-	-	-	-	-
satirise	4	>0.01	10	0.02	18	0.02	-
satirize	49	0.05	252	0.62	580	0.58	3457
savage	114	0.12	287	0.71	683	0.69	3939
savagize	-	-	-	-	-	-	-
scenario	-	-	-	-	-	-	-
scenarioize	-	-	-	-	-	-	-
scenarize	-	-	-	-	-	-	-
signal	303	0.31	4160	10.27	15998	16.11	168833
signalise	13	0.01	-	-	-	-	-
signalize	923	0.93	110	0.27	8	0.01	-
smart	1652	1.67	697	1.72	872	0.88	5203
smarten	-	-	46	0.11	211	0.21	2067

	EHCB		COHA		COCA		iWeb
	raw	per mil	raw	per mil	raw	per mil	
soft	223	0.23	-	-	-	-	-
soften	3709	3.76	6104	15.07	9017	9.08	110498
sonnet	70	0.07	-	-	-	-	-
sonnetize	-	-	-	-	-	-	-
soul	585	-	7	0.02	-	-	-
soulify	0.59	-	-	-	-	-	-
spruce	87	0.09	472	1.17	1007	1.01	18640
sprucify	1	>0.01	-	-	-	-	-
stark	95	0.1	-	-	-	-	-
starken	-	-	-	-	-	-	-
station	129	0.13	3833	9.46	5207	5.24	50808
stationize	1	>0.01	-	-	-	-	-
statue	5	0.01	-	-	-	-	-
statufy	-	-	-	-	-	-	-
strength	21152	21.43	-	-	-	-	-
strengthen	-	-	10188	25.16	21276	21.43	393931
substantify	-	-	-	-	-	-	-
substantize	-	-	-	-	-	-	-
summer	37	0.04	291	0.72	717	0.72	15836
summerize	-	-	-	-	4	0	-
terrify	9168	9.29	3792	9.36	9985	10.06	72202
terror	-	-	-	-	-	-	-
trust	48410	49.04	30723	75.86	77728	78.27	73965
trusten	8	0.01	-	-	-	-	-
union	-	-	1	-	-	-	-
unionize	-	-	86	0.21	395	0.4	-
valuate	1	>0.01	-	-	10	0.01	148
value	19703	19.96	5193	12.82	16523	16.64	314200
verb	-	-	-	-	-	-	-
verbify	-	-	-	-	-	-	-

	EHCB		COHA		COCA		iWeb
	raw	per mil	raw	per mil	raw	per mil	
verbal	0	0	-	-	-	-	-
verbalize	4	>0.01	83	0.2	1	0.61	5186
wanton	2262	2.29	-	-	-	-	-
wantonise	6	0.01	-	-	-	-	-
wantonize	49	0.05	-	-	-	-	-
white	773	0.78	1	0	-	-	-
whiten	947	0.96	970	2.4	719	0.72	21466
woman	6440	6.52	-	-	-	-	-
womanize	6	0.01	2	0	11	0.01	-

Figures

Tables

Author Index

Subject Index

Hallesche Sprach- und Textforschung
Language and Text Studies
Recherches linguistiques et textuelles

Herausgegeben von / Edited by / Dirigée par Alexander Brock & Daniela Pietrini

Bd./Vol. 1 Annette Schiller: Die présentatifs im heutigen Französisch. Eine funktionale Studie ihrer Vielfalt. 1992.

Bd./Vol. 2 Gertrud Bense (Hrsg.): Diachronie – Kontinuität – Impulse. Sprachwissenschaftliches Kolloquium Halle 1992. 1994.

Bd./Vol. 3 Wolfgang Boeck (Hrsg.): Sprache, Literatur und Landeskunde slavischer Völker. Funktionale Aspekte in der Beschreibung und Didaktik. 1994.

Bd./Vol. 4 Gertrud Bense (Hrsg.): Kommunikation und Grammatik. 1996.

Bd./Vol. 5 Gisela Hermann-Brennecke / Dietmar Schneider (Hrsg.): Dona Anglica. 120 Jahre Anglistik in Halle. 1997.

Bd./Vol. 6 Max Hans-Jürgen Mattusch: Vielsprachigkeit: Fluch oder Segen für die Menschheit? Zu Fragen einer europäischen und globalen Fremdsprachenpolitik. 1999.

Bd./Vol. 7 Christiane Schiller: Bilinguismus. Zur Darstellung eines soziolinguistischen Phänomens in der Literatur. Dargestellt an Beispielen der regionalen Literatur Preußisch-Litauens: Her- mann Sudermann *Litauische Geschichten*, Ieva Simonaityte *Vilius Karalius*. 2000.

Bd./Vol. 8 Gertrud Bense: „Giedojam taw – Wir singen dir". Zur Textgeschichte der preußisch-litauischen Gesangbücher im 18. Jahrhundert. Mit besonderer Berücksichtigung der Liedersammlung von Fabian Ulrich Glaser (1688–1747) und ihrem Umfeld. 2001.

Bd./Vol. 9 Gertrud Bense / Gerhard Meiser / Edeltraud Werner (Hrsg.): August Friedrich Pott. Beiträge der Halleschen Tagung anlässlich des zweihundertsten Geburtstages von August Friedrich Pott (1802–1887). 2005.

Bd./Vol. 10 Julia Balakina: Anglicisms in Russian and German Blogs. A Comparative Analysis. 2011.

Bd./Vol. 11 Thomas Bremer/Annette Schiller (Hrsg.): Dialekt und Standardsprache in Italien und Europa. Edeltraud Werner zum 60. Geburtstag. 2012.

Bd./Vol. 12 Anne Ammermann / Alexander Brock / Jana Pflaeging / Peter Schildhauer (eds.): Facets of Linguistics. Proceedings of the 14th Norddeutsches Linguistisches Kolloquium 2013 in Halle an der Saale. 2013.

Bd./Vol. 13 Anja Neuber: Perspektiven des Friaulischen. Eine soziolinguistische Untersuchung am Beispiel junger Erwachsener. 2015.

Bd./Vol. 14 Peter Schildhauer: The Personal Weblog. A Linguistic History. 2016.

Bd./Vol. 15 Alexander Brock / Peter Schildhauer (eds.): Communication Forms and Communicative Practices. New Perspectives on Communication Forms, Affordances and What Users Make of Them. 2017.

Bd./Vol. 16 Alexander Brock / Jana Pflaeging / Peter Schildhauer (eds.): Genre Emergence. Developments in Print, TV and Digital Media. 2019.

Bd./Vol. 17 Björn Langkopf: Autonomes E-Learning. Effizienz – Didaktik – Perspektiven. 2019.

Bd./Vol. 18 John Marcus Sommer: English and French Online Comments. A Text Linguistic Comparison of Popular Science Magazines. 2020.

Bd./Vol. 19 José Luis Oncins Martínez (ed.): Current Trends in Corpus Linguistics. 2020.

Bd./Vol. 20 Ramón Martí Solano / Pablo Ruano San Segundo (eds.): Anglicisms and Corpus Linguistics. Corpus-Aided Research into the Influence of English on European Languages. 2021.

Bd./Vol. 21 Cristina Fernández-Alcaina: The Competition of Word-Formation Processes in the Derivational Paradigm of Verbs. Diasynchronic Evidence for the Profile and Resolution of Competition in English. 2021.

www.peterlang.com

www.ingramcontent.com/pod-product-compliance
Ingram Content Group UK Ltd.
Pitfield, Milton Keynes, MK11 3LW, UK
UKHW010948270525
2059IPUK00016B/5

9 783631 866108